About The Authors

M. A. Madigan (New York) is currently a full-time stay-at-home father of one. Before his daughter was born, he was an intellectual engaged in the search for knowledge and an understanding of the physical and metaphysical worlds. Now he routinely tries to understand questions like, "What is it that makes throwing half of all the silverware in the house into the garbage fun?"

P. M. Richards (New York) was raised in the spiritualist tradition while in private, and as a member of the Episcopalian church while in public, so he describes himself as an "Episco-pagan." He resides in Buffalo, N.Y., where he is an active member of the large western New York pagan community. He is currently working on rendering all seventy-two demons from Solomon's *Goetia* into computer-generated portraits.

M. A. Madigan & P. M. Richards

Symbols
of the
Craft

2003
Llewellyn Publications
St. Paul, Minnesota 55164-0383, U.S.A.

FIRST EDITION
First Printing, 2003

Book design and editing by Rebecca Zins
Cover design and doohickies by Lisa Novak
Interior stone symbols by Llewellyn Art Department

Library of Congress Cataloging-in-Publication Data
Madigan, M. A., 1962–
    Symbols of the Craft / M. A. Madigan & P. M. Richards.—1st ed.
        p. cm.
    ISBN 0-7387-0194-7
    1. Divination. 2. Magic. 3. Charms. 4. Witchcraft.
        I. Richards, P. M., 1962– II. Title.

BF1773.M29 2003
133.3'22—dc21

                                                            2003047665

Llewellyn Worldwide does not participate in, endorse, or have any authority or responsibility concerning private business transactions between our authors and the public.

All mail addressed to the author is forwarded but the publisher cannot, unless specifically instructed by the author, give out an address or phone number.

Any Internet references contained in this work are current at publication time, but the publisher cannot guarantee that a specific location will continue to be maintained. Please refer to the publisher's website for links to authors' websites and other sources.

Llewellyn Publications
A Division of Llewellyn Worldwide, Ltd.
P.O. Box 64383, Dept. 0-7387-0194-7
St. Paul, MN 55164-0383, U.S.A.
www.llewellyn.com

Printed in the United States of America

Contents

Simple Spells, 99

Advanced Spells, 135

Preface

We created this book and the accompanying stones primarily as a divination method. We believe they will provide a means to help people begin to understand and touch the untapped energies slumbering within themselves.

When we chose to use the symbols of the ancient Craft—now often referred to as Wicca—as a divination method, we also created an excellent teaching aid and starting point for anyone interested in learning about the Craft. There are many fine books already available that explain the Craft in much greater detail than we could ever attempt here, and we do not claim that this book is the ultimate authority on the subject, only that it serves as a convenient starting point for novice witches and pagans.

In writing this book, we have chosen to use the words "witch" and "pagan" as interchangeable. While this may offend some pagans who do not consider themselves witches, and vice versa, it avoids the confusion that would have been caused trying to differentiate between the two groups, as definitions for these two words vary wildly in the traditions themselves. It has often been remarked that there are just as many definitions for the word "witch" as there are people who call themselves witches.

While researching this book, we gathered an incredible amount of conflicting information, as each pagan tradition seems, in varying degrees, to hold different beliefs. For example, some traditions will tell you that an esbat is strictly a full moon ceremony, while others insist that any non-sabbat ritual is technically an esbat, full moon or not. If you ask any three witches to define a "Book of Shadows," the first one will tell you that it's a record of coven activities, the second will say that it's a journal of your own personal growth, and the third will insist that you're wrong and it's actually called a "Mirror Book." The magical properties attributed to certain plants often vary from witch to witch as well, even when they live as neighbors within a small town.

This may be a source of confusion for novices, but this also demonstrates perfectly the concept that is at the heart of our pagan heritage: that it is the *intent* of the practitioner or spellcaster, not the physical format of the spell, that really matters.

No one tradition can be said to be more correct than any other, and we have tried to draw from as many sources as possible. In cases where conflicting information was gathered, we have attempted to provide as many differing viewpoints as seemed appropriate, without becoming overly confusing. We apologize if your particular beliefs are not represented here, but we welcome you to contact us regarding them.

Within the pages of this book you will find complete instructions on using the stones as a personal divination method. The stones may also be used as symbolic tools in the included rituals and spells. We have also provided some of the historic backgrounds of the symbols used on the stones to help you better understand their use in the Craft.

We hope that you find these stones to be helpful tools in your journey toward self-enlightenment, toward your discovery of yourself, and toward your discovery of the ancient Craft.

Blessed be to you all,

P. M. Richards & M. A. Madigan

A note on divination & spells

When seeking guidance from any oracle, it is important that the seeker and interpreter have as clear an understanding of the question to be asked as possible. If your question is half formed and tenuous, then your reading will share these characteristics. The clearer the interpreter's and seeker's understanding of the question, the more helpful and easier your readings will be.

Furthermore, the divinities have knowledge of all things and wisdom beyond measure. We, as mortals, do not. Sometimes we may seek guidance on one matter and the deities will answer an unspoken or unthought-of question instead. If your reading doesn't appear to answer the question you've asked, an attempt to uncover the matter that the deities have chosen to address is usually indicated. In many cases, the advice we asked for turns out not to be the advice we actually need.

Please note that there are no special reverse meanings to these stones, as an inverse Sun stone would look exactly like a normal one, as would the Goddess, Salt, Rebirth, Full Moon, New Moon, etc. There is also no blank stone, as these stones are not just another set of rune stones.

Also, remember that it is always up to the individual interpreting the stone layouts to determine the final meaning of each stone in a reading. If this book says that a stone stands for "harmony in life" but you feel certain that it should stand for discord, then of course, for you, it means "discord" in your reading.

Interpreting mystical symbols is an art form, and all art is an expression of the individual. Just as all painters have access to the same colors of paint, yet they don't all paint the same picture, so it is with oracular interpretation. The mood, attitude, and general state of mind of the interpreter can, and should, affect the nature and character of the layout and the meanings derived from it.

If you are in a bad mood and just don't care, then your stone spread will reflect this attitude and color your reading. This is why creating a small personal ritual, performed prior to consulting with your stones, is a good idea. The performance of a ritual allows your mind to tune out the distractions of the mundane forces that tug at your everyday existence and focus more clearly on the stones and the layout before you.

We have included a short ritual for cleansing extraneous energies prior to readings, ceremonies, and spells (see page xxi). We also advise that you familiarize yourself fully with the definitions, use, and position of each stone prior to attempting any spells, rituals, or readings.

To realize the full potential of the stones, especially when spellcasting, it is necessary to understand why each specific stone has been placed in its particular position, and what that stone in that position symbolically represents. Not knowing why each symbol is used could result in less than satisfactory results.

In the writing of our spells we have deliberately avoided using ancient-sounding words of power or the names of obscure and nearly unpronounceable deities. The reason for this is simple. In order to properly perform spells or rituals, you must fully understand what it is you are doing. If part of your mind is focused on remembering how to pronounce "Glasya-Labolas," "Marchosias," "Amdusias," and "Decarabia," then you will be unable to concentrate your personal energy on your desired goals.

You may use the spells, rituals, and readings we have provided in whole or in part, as is or modified. Better yet, you may devise entirely new ritual practices of your own with your stones. As with all things magical, the choice is always yours.

Finally, be aware that casting spells on other people has consequences. Trying to change someone else with your own energy will fail 99 percent of the time. Save your energy, and change yourself instead. This is much more likely to produce the results you desire. Even if your spell does work, manipulating someone through magic without their consent is a violation of one of the basic premises of Wicca: that no matter what you do, you should harm no one, including yourself. You cannot foresee all of the long-term consequences of your castings, so your spells may cause great harm, even if the change you elicit may seem beneficial in the short term. Also, using your energy to influence someone else will leave you open and vulnerable to the same type of influence from outside, times three, that you attempt on someone else.

Most Wiccans and other pagans agree in the validity of the Threefold Law, which states that the energy we put out comes back to us three times stronger, so weigh the consequences carefully before deciding to cast upon someone other than yourself.

Charging your stones

Your energy gives the stones purpose and direction. Prior to using them, you should charge your new stones with your own personal energy. Through you, the stones derive their ability to speak to your desires.

To charge your stones, begin by selecting a suitable location—a place where you will not be disturbed. Once you have selected your location, create your sacred space (see page xxi). Lay out the stones facedown, and recite the following Invocation to the Elements:

In my circle, reverently cast,
Safe from curse or psychic blast,
From sea and desert, hill and glade,
By cup and wand, by salt and blade,
Water and air, earth and fire,
Elements of my worldly desire,
I invoke you now to listen to me.
This is my will, so mote it be!

Place one stone facedown in the palm of your right hand (or your left, if it is more comfortable for you). Now visualize your own energy swirling together like a tiny whirlpool of light, hovering just above the stone. Let your energy flow into the whirlpool until the image becomes clear in your mind. While holding this clear image firmly in your mind, repeat the last two lines of the Invocation to the Elements:

I invoke you now to listen to me.
This is my will, so mote it be!

As you speak the words, visualize your energy diving into the stone in your palm, spreading itself throughout the stone and energizing it. Now place your stone into the pouch and repeat this process with the next stone, until you have energized and placed into the bag all thirty-five of the stones.

When all of your stones are inside the pouch, put the pouch into the space that the stones originally occupied. Repeat again the entire Invocation to the Elements. When you have done this, close the pouch and thank the elements for their assistance.

Now disperse your sacred space (see page xxiii). Your stones are now energized and ready for your use. May they aid you in your search for truth and understanding.

Preparing layout space

Wherever people gather, they unintentionally leave behind psychic energy. This residue can quickly build up and negatively influence a reading or the working of other magic, so it will need to be cleansed prior to starting. This will help to avoid the corruption of your reading or crafting. Prepare your layout space before working any spell or ritual with the stones.

Required stones:
- ⋆ Besom
- ⋆ Athame
- ⋆ Wand

You will first need to create what is known as a magic circle or sacred space. This is a nonphysical sphere of personal power that envelops the practitioner and contains the practitioner's magical energies during readings, rituals, and spells. When completed, you should actually be able to feel this sphere around you.

First, ritually cleanse the area you will be using. Begin by holding the Besom stone in one hand and, using a sweeping motion, move it from the center of the area outward, as if you were actually sweeping with an ordinary whiskbroom. With each pass of the Besom stone, imagine it brushing away extraneous energies like motes of dust, and say:

I cleanse this space of energies forgotten.

Do this until you have cleansed the entire area that your circle will occupy. Use as many or as few strokes as you feel are needed, but be sure that your strokes are always from the center pushing outward, and that each following stroke is made in a widdershins (counterclockwise) progression around the area. This is to clear away any excess energies that may interfere with your casting. When you have finished, put the Besom stone away.

Your layout area is now free of diluting energies and can be used for the rest of your crafting.

Magic circle

To create your magic circle, hold the Athame stone in one hand (the right hand if you are right-handed) and the Wand stone in the other. Create your magic circle by walking deosil (clockwise) around the area you will be using while pointing the Athame stone and the Wand stone toward the ground to define the boundaries of your magic circle. If space is limited, you may stand in the center of your circle and simply turn deosil while pointing the Athame. You may also mark your circle with a ring of stones, a piece of string, or a ribbon on the surface you will be using, but this is optional.

Envision the sphere of sacred space forming around you from your own energies. Continue walking or turning deosil until you've gathered what you feel is sufficient energy for your needs.

If you have special deities that you honor, now is the time to invite them to attend and witness your circle along with the Goddess and the God. Your circle will be complete when you feel their presence in the circle with you.

Dispersing layout space

When you have finished your reading, spell, or ritual, you will need to disperse your sacred space. Thank your deities for attending, and then walk or turn widdershins (counterclockwise) while you draw the energy of your magic circle back into yourself. Envision your sphere gradually collapsing into you. If you marked your circle in some way, remove the markings now. Your circle is now dispersed.

Divination Methods

Three-stone draw

Concentrate on the question you wish your quick reading to address. When you have formed your question clearly in your mind, carefully and thoroughly mix the stones around. This may be done by spreading them facedown in front of you, or by shaking them thoroughly in the drawstring pouch.

After they are mixed, pick up the first stone your finger touches and lay it faceup in position one, as shown in the diagram below. Do not stop to examine the stone at this time, but immediately pick your next stone, and lay it faceup in position two, then pick your third stone and place it in position three. You are now ready to begin your reading.

position one: This is something that is over and done with in your life. It is something that has already happened and cannot be altered by any future actions, but it will have direct bearing on your question. Use the past meaning of this symbol.

position two: This is something that is already here. It's part of your current life experience, and although this thing's connection may be hidden or disguised, it will have a profound influence over your situation as it relates to your question. Look for this connection to understand this stone. Use the present meaning of this symbol.

position three: This is the most likely outcome to your question. The reader must take into account all of the information revealed by the two previous stones when reading this position, or its relation to your question may be easily misinterpreted. Use the future meaning of this symbol.

The bane method

Create your sacred space as described in the "Preparing Layout Space" section on page xxi.

Lay all thirty-five of your stones facedown on the surface in front of you, and concentrate on the question you wish your reading to address. When you have formed your question clearly in your mind, carefully and thoroughly mix the stones. After they are mixed, pick up and place six stones faceup, one at a time, in the order shown in the diagram below. Make sure to move only deosil (clockwise) around the pattern.

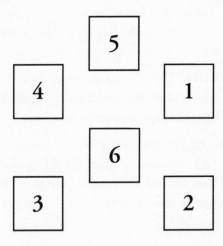

Interpret the stones according to the following guidelines. Be certain that you fully understand the meaning of each piece, as it relates in its position within the layout, before moving on to the next position.

position one: This is over and done with. It is something that has already happened and cannot be altered by any future actions. Read from the past position meaning.

position two: This is on the way out. This is a thing that is currently present in your life and not yet a part of your past, but soon will be. Read from either the past or the present position meaning.

position three: This is on the way in. This is a new thing that is soon to enter into your life. Read from either the present or the future position meaning.

position four: This is something that will happen to you in the future. When it will occur is up to the Goddess and the God to decide. Read from the future position meaning.

position five: This is what is already here. It's part of your current experience and has bearing on the matter. Read from the present position meaning.

position six: This is the most likely outcome. The reader must take into account all of the things that have already been revealed when reading this stone. Read from the future position meaning.

New moon layout

The New Moon Layout does not seek to foretell the future. It serves instead as a guide in your search for the correct path.

Create your sacred space as described in the "Preparing Layout Space" section on page xxi.

Lay all thirty-five of the witching stones facedown on the surface in front of you. Concentrate on the choices for which you seek guidance. Imagine them as pathways leading into darkness. When you have the image firmly in your mind, speak the following invocation:

Goddess, Mother, Wizened Crone,
I seek for truth, let truth be known.

Now carefully and thoroughly mix the stones. When the stones are thoroughly mixed, have the questioner, be it you or another person, pick four stones and lay them out, faceup, in the positions shown on page 8. Be sure to pick up and place them one at a time.

The following guidelines should be followed when reading the stones in this layout. An understanding of the symbol's description and its divinatory meanings is essential before continuing on to the next position. Use the present position meanings for all of these positions.

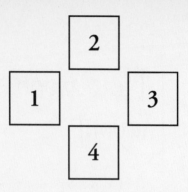

position one represents the spiritual as well as the physical nature of the person seeking guidance. As humans we wear the aspects of both spiritual and physical beings. It is essential to understand the dual aspect of our beings before we can begin to fully understand ourselves.

position two represents the nature of the problem. It stands for the matter that the questioner is seeking guidance for. If the deities have chosen to answer a question different from the one asked, then that question would be indicated here.

position three represents the obstacles that are preventing any further understanding. If a stone of positive meaning shows up here, you should consider carefully before you reverse its meaning. Sometimes good things do stand between you and your true desires and needs.

position four represents the source of the needed knowledge. It is the path to understanding and eventual enlightenment. However, it is not necessarily the easiest path to follow. Seldom is the easy path a rewarding experience. A journey around the mountain in a motor vehicle does not teach the same lessons as the climb on foot over the top does.

Magic circle layout

A good layout for advanced practitioners

Create your sacred space as described in the "Preparing Layout Space" section.

Lay all thirty-five of the witching stones facedown on the surface in front of you. Thoroughly mix the stones, then have the questioner, be it you or another person, pick nine stones and lay them out facedown in the positions shown here. Be sure to pick up and place them facedown one at a time, and only then, once all nine have been selected, turn them over one by one.

The following guidelines should be followed when reading the stones in this layout. An understanding of the symbol's description and its divinatory meanings is always essential before continuing on to reveal the next position. Use the present position meanings for all of these positions.

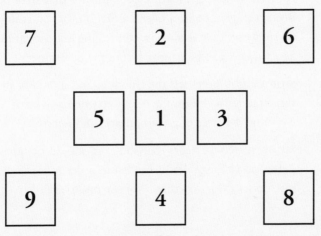

position one represents the pentacle, and stands for the person who is seeking guidance or knowledge.

position two represents the element of earth, and stands for the nature of the problem or the matter that the questioner is seeking guidance about.

position three represents the element of air, and stands for obstacles that are preventing further understanding.

position four represents the element of fire, and stands for some sort of change that is necessary to gain understanding, or the knowledge needed to achieve understanding.

position five represents the element of water, and therefore stands for cleansing. This stone may represent a person or thing that needs to be removed from the questioner's life in order for future growth to occur, or something that needs to be added for the same reason.

position six represents the wand, and stands for something that should be invited into the questioner's life.

position seven represents the athame, and stands for control. This is something or someone that may be needed to gain control over a situation, or something or someone that is already controlling the situation, and may need to be removed from the questioner's life.

position eight represents the Goddess, and should be interpreted as the lesson the questioner needs to learn to continue the cycle of growth, death, and rebirth.

position nine represents the God, and should be interpreted as a change that is needed in order to teach the questioner the lesson that he or she must learn.

The Stones

Altar

An altar may be an elaborate permanent structure, a simple tree stump in the woods, or even a cardboard box for a spur-of-the-moment ritual. The actual object is immaterial; as with most crafting, it is the intent that is important. If you create a permanent altar it will be a personal object, and yours need only be pleasing to you.

The Goddess and God don't inhabit the altar, of course, but it is believed by many traditions to be a place of accumulated power and magic, and it is usually found at the center of every magic circle.

To make your altar you can use any material, but wood is usually considered to be the best as it is a good conductor of magical energies. An altar made of willow wood honors the Goddess, but oak, for the God, will lend its strength to your rites and spells. Special woods, like apple or elder, may also be used if they have a special significance to your magic or gods.

Ritual tools are usually placed on the altar prior to creating the sacred space surrounding the practitioner. The left side of the altar is usually reserved for the Goddess. According to many traditions, the besom, chalice, pentacle, and cauldron are often considered to be objects dedicated to the Goddess, so should be placed there. The right half of the altar is reserved for the God, so the athame, censer, wand, and candle are usually placed there. In some traditions the cauldron, censer, and pentacle are placed in the center of the altar instead of their respective sides, while others reserve this center area as a sort of working space. As with all crafting, specifics vary greatly from tradition to tradition.

past position: A lack of cooperation in the past is hurting a current project. You may have been the uncooperative one, or it may have been someone or something else that was the problem. It doesn't matter. Until there is compromise, the stalemate will continue.

present position: An opportunity for unity through cooperation is about to present itself, but it will be disguised as something entirely different. Examine all new events with this in mind, and you will spot it immediately when it comes.

future position: You will need unity through cooperation soon, so start working in that direction now. Be the glue that binds the book and great rewards will await you. If you fail to gain cooperation now, things will soon begin to fall apart.

Athame

Also called a "magic knife," this tool is rarely if ever used for cutting, but instead is used for the directing of personal power that is raised during rituals and spells toward the accomplishment of specific goals. It is most commonly a double-edged knife with a black or dark handle, as it is believed by many that the dark handle will store excess energy generated during rituals for later use in spellcastings or other magic.

If something must be cut for magical purposes outside of the magic circle, a small branch to make a wand, or herbs to be mixed with wine, for instance, many modern pagans will use a bolline, or white-handled knife. Usually a sharp kitchen knife that has been dedicated solely to magic purposes will serve as a bolline, provided that it can do the cutting efficiently. Other traditions hold that the bolline must never be used outside of a magic circle, and some even inscribe mystical symbols and sigils on the blades of their magic knives.

Unlike the wand, many believe that the athame should never be used to invoke, but to command. As an instrument of command it should never be directed toward the Goddess, the God or any other deities, but used solely to direct your own personal power to accomplish your desired goal. To presume to command the deities would indeed be a great offense.

Some traditions use the athame to create the magic circle instead of a wand, often pointing the blade toward the earth as they slowly walk deosil to gather energy. Some use it almost like a magic pointer to create pentacles in the air over each of the four compass points. It can be used to represent the element of fire when placed on the eastern side of the altar, or it can be used to "cut" a temporary entrance or exit to the magic circle in case of unexpected events, or the need for breaks during long ceremonies. In short, the use of the athame in ritual magic is almost limitless.

It is not clear when the athame was first introduced into ritual magic, but its use in pagan ceremonies and rituals can be observed throughout most of recorded history all over the world. Many traditions disagree on specifics, but the athame is believed by most to be linked to the element of fire, as it brings about change. A consecrated sword can be used as an athame, but can be unwieldy in small spaces and difficult to store between rituals.

past position: This stone can be seen as a time when you made a poor choice and directed your personal power into frivolous purposes. This may have been in the form of the fruitless pursuit of another person, or just time wasted in leisure activities that could have been used more productively. Learn from the past, and use your remaining time wisely.

present position: You may be sincerely trying to redirect your personal power into more constructive avenues, but something is holding you back. The source of the problem is plainly visible in your daily life. Open your eyes and look around you. You may be very surprised that you didn't see it before.

future position: This stone indicates that properly directed personal energy used for constructive purposes is in your future. It may be that the energy is someone else's or your own, but it will be intentionally directed to be to your benefit. Look for this to happen when you need it most.

Autumn

The first of the autumn sabbats is Lugh-nasadh, Lammas, or August Eve, celebrated on August 1. This day historically marked the first harvest, and was a time for celebration by one and all. As the crops were brought in from the fields and stored against the winter shortages, there was time for a little relaxation. Seeds were gathered and stored for use in the planting season the following spring, ensuring the continued cycle of life.

As the sun begins to lose its strength in autumn, so too does the God. The nights begin to lengthen, and he knows it is just a matter of time now before his inevitable decline. The Goddess is saddened by his state, but they both take joy in the fact that he will continue on as his own seed inside the Goddess. His rebirth is as inevitable as spring.

The food from the autumn harvest should remind us of the abundance of summer, even when we eat in the dead of winter. It is a physical symbol of the never-ending cycle of rebirth.

Mabon is the next sabbat, and occurs on the autumn equinox in late September, when once again the days and nights are in balance. The harvest begun at Lughnasadh has been finished, and the abundance of the earth has begun to wane as the plants and animals alike ready themselves for the coming winter.

This is a time of rest after the harvest, symbolized by the pregnant Goddess lying in the weakening sun. She can feel the God growing ever stronger inside her, even as he grows weaker next to her. His death is now just a matter of time, as soon he must abandon his physical body and wait for his renewal through rebirth from the Goddess.

This is a time for introspection, giving thanks, and making peace for most pagans.

past position: This is a time in your past when change, great or small, was necessary. It may have been a painful or a joyful change, but it was something that you now realize was absolutely necessary, otherwise you would not be the person that you are now.

present position: Now is the time for necessary change, great or small, so don't shy away from it. Grab the bull by the horns and run with it, or else you will be quickly trampled.

future position: Soon the time will be right for necessary change, great or small, but not yet. Wait for it. You will know when the time is right to make your move.

Balefire

Any fire lit for magical purposes can be considered a balefire, but traditionally it is an outdoor fire to illuminate a ritual, especially to celebrate Beltane, Midsummer, or Yule.

Some practitioners insist on the need for "nine sacred woods" (oak and eight other woods) to build their balefire, while others couldn't care less what materials are used. Some of the woods that are commonly used to construct a balefire are apple, ash, birch, cedar, juniper, pine, poplar, rowan and, of course, oak as the base. If these are unavailable in your area, most native woods also are considered acceptable alternatives.

There are exceptions to every rule, of course. For example, a balefire composed entirely of driftwood collected along the shore can be used to illuminate a rite or ceremony conducted on a beach or shoreline. This can also add a mystical air to your ritual, especially if the driftwood was taken from salt water, and sparkles with colored flames from the burning sea salts.

Often a pouch of incense will be placed into the balefire, either before or after lighting, to add sweet scents to the already magical tableau. If you are using strongly scented woods for your balefire, make sure the incense is designed to complement the scent of the wood, and not compete against it.

Leaping over the balefire is an ancient custom believed to bring good fortune to all. Often celebrants will wait until the balefire is little more than embers to do this, but others find leaping a roaring fire to be much more exciting. Either way, precautions to avoid catching any clothing on fire should always be taken. The tradition of jumping the balefire skyclad (nude) has regained popularity in recent years. Holding hands with your partner while you both leap the Beltane balefire is believed to bring fertility, and children conceived immediately after are thought to be especially blessed.

past position: This represents a simpler time in your life when your belief in the world's magic was clear. It may have been many years ago, or just last week, but it was a time when you were in awe of the natural world around you. Hang on to that feeling of magic and wonder, regardless of others who will try to convince you that you are wrong.

present position: This symbol usually indicates a need for closer examination of a basic belief. Often the belief in question will be clouded by many other peoples' perspectives, so be careful to weed through all the noise around you in order to hear the true meaning you seek.

future position: There will be an internal struggle in your near future. Many different choices will be given to you, and the correct path will remain clouded. When the crisis occurs, think back to a time in your past when you believed without question in the magic that you see all around you, and you will know what to do.

Bane

The word "bane" is simply an old word for "bad," as in "all that you do, good or bane, shall return to you threefold."

The bane symbolizes all the things that generate negative energy. Many pagans will argue that there is no such thing as negative energy, and that it is how the energy is directed that is negative. This is a matter of contention between some traditions, but in either case everything that destroys life and is poisonous, destructive, evil, or malicious can be considered a bane, and should be avoided by the modern-day witch according to the vast majority of traditions.

Every now and again you will meet someone who will tell you that there is no real harm in making curses and spells that will hurt other people. Do not believe them.

Keep in mind the rule of three, which states that the energies we put out, both positive and negative, will come back to us threefold. Therefore beware of negative energy in any form, and never use negative energy in your crafting. There is a great quote by Scott Cunningham under the Widdershins stone about the Rule of Three or Threefold Law that you should also consult.

past position: This symbol can be interpreted as a bad habit that should have been eliminated long ago, but you've never believed yourself strong enough to break away. You're stronger than you know, and soon the time will be right to rid yourself of this thing.

present position: This represents self-destructive behavior that should be eliminated. It could be drinking to excess, drugs, promiscuity, an addiction to another person, or a host of other sources of negative energy. Rid your life of them soon, or the consequences will be long lasting and far reaching.

future position: You will soon encounter a negative influence from outside that will attempt to derail you. This influence should not be challenged, but should be avoided at all costs. If you believe you can win against it, then you have already lost this struggle. Steer clear of this influence and you will prosper.

Besom

This is the most-recognized symbol of witchcraft: the magic broom.

While the idea of a witch riding a broom through the sky during a full moon is certainly humorous to the modern witch, it may have been handed down to us as a metaphor by people who simply did not understand astral projection, as it may have been practiced by the ancients. Some scholars believe that the myth may have originated with certain fertility rites, during which women would hop through the fields with a broom between their legs, like a child's toy horse, to ensure a good crop. However the myth was started, it has endured to the present day.

The besom is used to ritually cleanse an area of all psychic residue prior to rituals. The besom doesn't have to touch the floor at all, but the wielder should visualize the bristles clearing away any negativity or extraneous energy as they sweep the area from the center outward prior to setting up the altar.

Historically it has been used to guard against negative energy when placed across a doorway or over a window. This was believed to protect all those within from curses, spells, and other forms of evil.

Many modern witches and pagans prefer a handfasting ceremony as opposed to a modern traditional wedding, where the couple will still jump over a besom to seal the union. This is actually quite an ancient practice, used by the Romanies (Gypsies) for centuries, as well as by many other cultures throughout history.

The traditional besom has an ash staff for protection, birch bristles for purifying, and willow bindings to honor the Goddess, but many commercially made besoms are available in a wide variety of woods and other materials.

As a purifying tool, it is linked to the element of water, and it is sacred to both the Goddess and the God. Obviously, your besom should never be used for mundane cleaning chores.

past position: This indicates a time of purity and innocence, now forever lost. There may have been a definite moment in your life when that innocence was shattered, or it may just have slowly worn away. Either way, the loss of innocence doesn't have to mean the loss of wonder at the universe around us. Try to see the big picture and recapture a portion of that purity and innocence.

present position: This usually indicates a need for cleansing yourself spiritually and letting go of something that's holding you down, or a need to purify your surroundings and purge them of residual negative energy left by other people. Often it can indicate a need for both. You will not be able to reach your desired goals until you cleanse away the things that are keeping you back.

future position: This stone can always be seen as a warning when in the future position of a reading, but the nature of the warning can often be obscure until examined after the fact. Prepare for an unexpected change in the near future, and remember that forewarned is not necessarily forearmed.

Candle

Candles are used for a variety of purposes in ritual magic. In addition to lending a mysterious and exotic air to your surroundings, they are an exquisite way to illuminate your rituals when a balefire is impractical. They are often used on the altar to represent the Goddess and the God, and at the compass points of a magic circle to represent the four elements.

Many traditions believe that you should never blow out a candle, as this can be construed as using air (wind) to insult fire, and both elements may become offended. Instead you should use a candle snuffer, or preferably pinch the wick between your thumb and finger to extinguish the flame. A few traditions maintain that you should never light a ritual candle with a lighter or a match, but instead light a taper specifically for lighting other candles. As with most things in magic, it seems to be mostly the intent of the person who is using the candle that matters, and not how the candle is lit or extinguished.

A store-bought candle works fine, although some witches prefer ornate figurines and expensive hand-dipped or sand-cast works of art for their altars. Candles have always been readily available in a wide variety of sizes, shapes, scents, and colors, but recently special "pre-spelled" candles have appeared. These are sold already made with herbs mixed into the wax and inscriptions pre-etched, claiming to be designed to accomplish specific purposes. Most modern witches and pagans still prefer to cast their own spells, though.

A common spell for removing a negative influence involves affixing a specially prepared black candle to the bottom of your cauldron and then adding water from your chalice until the candle is half submerged. Once the candle is lit, the practitioner should meditate quietly within the magic circle on the nature of the negative influence until the burning candle extinguishes itself. This could vary between a few minutes and a few days, depending on the candle. Candle wax can burn at drastically different rates, and you should be aware of this if you use candles in casting your spells.

Most traditions hold that the color of each candle can have a very specific meaning, which varies from tradition to tradition. In general it can be said that softer, earth-toned colors like blue and green are most commonly used to honor the Goddess, while the louder colors, like red and yellow, are reserved for the God.

Infusing candles with a purpose by inscribing detailed sigils prior to their ritual use is an ancient practice that is still used by most traditions today. The symbols and inscriptions that are used vary widely, of course.

past position: The candle in a past position stands for a time when some major event occurred and you really needed to give thanks to the deities. It may be that you missed this opportunity to give thanks entirely, or that you joyfully gave honor to the Goddess, the God, and your personal deities. Either way, this event was a turning point in your life, and it had a very special significance to you. Think about it for a while, and you will understand how that event relates to the rest of your reading.

present position: This stone indicates a need to thank your own personal deities. Something has recently occurred in your life that may not seem like a good thing right now, but it will turn out to be to your benefit in the long run. Give thanks as soon as possible to hasten your understanding of the true nature of the situation.

future position: There is a coming need for giving thanks to the deities. This represents an event that will have a major impact on your life, but may not be readily apparent to you at first. You will recognize it immediately when you do finally notice it, so be sure to remain humble and give thanks for your good fortune.

Cauldron

This is any container in which a magical transformation occurs, but traditionally it is usually a three-legged cast-iron kettle whose mouth is narrower than its widest bulge at the middle. The cauldron has been associated with witches since long before Shakespeare's fictional fates toiled over their bubbling cauldron, and is now an almost universal symbol of witchcraft. Surprisingly, they are quite easy to find in a variety of sizes at almost any New Age store.

The cauldron is linked to the element of water and it can symbolize the holy spring, inspiration, or the sea of creation. Some ceremonies involve setting a balefire within the cauldron, while others involve filling it with water, so your cauldron needs to be versatile and durable.

It is usually placed on the left side of the altar along with the pentacle and chalice to honor the Goddess, but if it is too large to fit there it may also be placed on the floor to the left of the altar. Some traditions hold that the cauldron should be the focal point of rituals, always taking center place on the altar.

Ancient Beltane celebrations often use the obviously symbolic gesture of inserting the masculine wand into the feminine chalice to ensure fertility of the land. This sexual symbolism lives on to this day in many traditions.

A common spell for removing negative influences involves dedicating a black candle to the influences you wish to be rid of, affixing the candle to the inside bottom of the cauldron, filling the cauldron with water, and allowing the candle to burn down to where it will eventually extinguish itself. You can also fill a cauldron with water and scry (gaze) into its depths to receive insights and visions.

past position: This represents something that you experienced, but you just couldn't explain. Think back to this incident and re-examine the past through the experiences you've had since, and you will find a link that you didn't know was there.

present position: This indicates that for a limited time an abundance of creative energy is available to you. Seize the opportunity and make an effort to think along unusual or uncommon lines, and your new insights will prove very fruitful indeed.

future position: Magic is in the air, and something wonderful is about to happen. It could be a spiritual awakening, a financial windfall, or anything else that will bring beneficial change into your life, so be ready when it happens or you may be overwhelmed.

Censer

Incense has been part of every major religion since time immemorial, and was originally believed by many cultures to help carry the prayers of devotees up to the spiritual plane, and to assist the spirits of the dead in their journey up to the gods. There are very few that still believe this to be the case; however, this ancient practice is still included in most modern rituals. In fact, many Catholic funeral services still conclude with the priest circling the coffin widdershins while swinging a censer to create clouds of incense smoke.

The use of incense and censers by the general public has skyrocketed in recent years, and a wide variety of scents and styles can now be conveniently purchased in most grocery stores, as well as in traditional metaphysical stores. Specialty incenses have become quite common, and are now sold under brand names like "Lotto Luck" or "Aphrodite's Passion" that are designed to accomplish specific goals, although many pagans still make their own incense if they wish to use it for magical purposes.

The popularity of incense may be due in part to the neurological properties of certain scents themselves. Modern scientists have demonstrated that many types of scents are able to influence our emotions directly, as the human sense of smell does not involve the thought process at all, but rather circumvents it to act on the emotional centers of the human brain directly. The ancients, who made use of incense in most rituals, were not ignorant of the psychological effects of these scents.

Incense can be purchased in a variety of forms, such as in cones, sticks, or less frequently in their traditional form of powders and resins. Censers now come in a huge variety of very creative styles, and can be purchased just about anywhere.

Today incense is used as an important aid in the mental preparation for a ritual, rather than as a required element of the ritual itself. Pleasantly scented incense burning in a censor can help to create a desired mental attitude, atmosphere, or mood.

Spirits are sometimes invoked to appear in the smoke rising from the censer, and the Goddess and the God can sometimes be seen peering at us through the twisting, curling incense smoke, but only if they choose to be seen.

Some witches place the censer on the right side of their altar to honor the God, while others will place it in the east to represent the element of air. Neither method is more correct than any other.

past position: This represents a personal revelation, something about yourself that you learned long ago. It was a painful lesson to learn, but you needed to learn it the hard way. You have since forgotten or have chosen to ignore it. Now is the time to bring it back into the light and re-examine what you once knew about yourself before it becomes necessary for you to learn this lesson all over again.

present position: You are missing something important right in front of you. There is a vital lesson that you need to learn in order to grow, but you can't see it from where you are at right now. It is time to change your view before this opportunity is lost to you forever. Seek to learn about yourself from what you see around you, and you will find the lesson that you need.

future position: In the future position this stone usually means a personal revelation is coming. This revelation may be in the form of a message from a friend, a gift, or some other form of communication that will lead you to special insight. Be very aware of your surroundings, or you may misinterpret or miss this message altogether.

Chalice

Much like a cauldron on a stem, the cup, goblet, or chalice can be used to symbolize the fertile Goddess nearing the Mother aspect, and may be considered an instrument of change.

A chalice is often placed on the west compass point of a magic circle to represent the element of water. The chalice is considered by most witches to be related to water since it is designed to hold liquids, although others will argue that since it represents change it should be linked to the element of fire. Neither belief is more correct than the other is, but water seems to be the prevailing favorite.

On the altar, the chalice is usually placed on the left side to honor the Goddess, along with the pentacle and cauldron. More practically, it is also used to hold water, wine, or some other ritual beverage for use during ceremonies. Often during group rituals, a chalice filled with wine and herbs will be passed around the circle of celebrants, and as each takes a sip they are bound together in a common purpose.

A plain wooden cup will work just as well as an ornate, pentacle-encrusted, silver-inlaid, long-stem leaded crystal masterpiece, but as always your altar need be pleasing to only one person: you.

past position: In a past position, this stone indicates a time of hesitation, where opportunities have been lost or neglected. Learn from your past mistakes, or you will be taught this lesson all over again soon.

present position: Heightened creativity, production, and personal power are readily available to you right now. Seize this opportunity and start a new spell or project as soon as possible, and the results will be especially fruitful.

future position: This indicates that a time of heightened creativity or personal power is approaching rapidly. The time for change will soon be at hand. Be prepared for anything, or you may be swept away in a tide of your own making.

Deosil

If you stand facing the sunrise and turn to follow the sun's apparent motion through the sky, you will turn clockwise, or deosil. Moving clockwise around the altar is one of the oldest magical traditions ever recorded, and is attributed by most to be a remnant of ancient sun magic.

This practice is still commonly used in most traditions to summon energy into a magic circle. Moving deosil around the altar is believed to generate positive energies by nearly every tradition, as widdershins is associated with dispersing negative energy, but everyone except for the most fanatic traditions agrees that if someone accidentally moves in the wrong direction around an altar it will not cause misfortune. As with all things magical, it is the intent of the person that really matters.

Switch the meaning of deosil with widdershins if you are in the Southern Hemisphere, because the apparent motion of the sun is reversed in your sky.

past position: This was a time when you learned to revere all life. It may have been as simple as watching a spider build her web, a trip to the zoo, or a chance encounter with wildlife, but there was certainly an animal involved. It was a time when you truly felt at peace and at one with nature.

present position: Good results can be obtained now if you seek the advice of others, but be careful whom you seek guidance from. Seek out an old friend you have not seen for a while for new insights and unexpected assistance.

future position: Other people will attempt to stand between you and the positive energy that you will need to obtain the results you desire. Arguing will not change their viewpoint, so don't even bother to try. The best path is to avoid them until you have the results you need.

Full moon

According to some traditions, esbats are rituals that must always be held on the full moon, while other belief systems maintain that any non-sabbat ritual can be called an esbat. In either case, ceremonies held on the night of the full moon are especially potent, as this is a night of power and a time of fulfillment, symbolized by the Goddess heavy with child. Many covens will schedule dedicated ritual circles for every full moon, while other groups prefer to be more spontaneous with their esbats and hold them whenever the mood strikes.

Just as the moon governs the cycles of the tides, so it also governs our human cycles. While our spells do not get their energy directly from the moon, when the moon is full it can often seem to increase the personal energy available to us, making the spells we cast and the rituals we perform that much more potent. In short, it is not the spell that gets stronger at the full moon, just the spellcaster.

While a full moon ritual should preferably be held on the exact night of the full moon, it's okay to hold it a few days before or after if the scheduling can't be arranged for everyone's convenience. Often the closest weekend to the full moon will do, and it is usually much more practical in today's busy working world to get people together on a weekend. Remember that it's always better to celebrate a few days early or late than to miss the opportunity for spellcrafting that the full moon presents.

past position: This stone represents a time in your past when you had an abundance of personal power. You will remember this time immediately, as well as its special significance to you. It also has special significance to the rest of your reading.

present position: This indicates that you are entering into a time of heightened personal power. You may expend this energy on pursuits that will make you happy immediately, or you may use this energy for more constructive purposes that will bear fruit later on. Either way, remember that all things come in cycles.

future position: This stone indicates that a time of heightened personal power will be upon you shortly. You may choose to enhance this future energy by casting spells and giving thanks to the deities now.

God

This is the symbol of the Horned God. Although he is eternally reborn of the Goddess, he is also her consort and her equal. Together they achieve balance and harmony while reflecting all the cycles of the Earth. As the Goddess is associated with the cycles of the moon, the God can be seen in the cycles of the sun—the four seasons.

He is associated with all the beasts of the Earth and with the hunt, thus the symbolic horns. This is in no way a reference or resemblance to the Christian "horned devil," which came about much later in history, possibly as negative propaganda against the Old Ways.

As the cycles of the moon are representations of the Goddess, the sun is the physical representation of the God. It governs the cycles of the seasons, but is also limited by them.

The infant God is born of the Goddess on Yule (again, not a reference to later Christian beliefs), and grows strong and true as the winter changes to spring.

By summer, he is depicted as a handsome adult man in his prime, full of life, strength, and lust. He pursues and wins the heart of the Goddess, and takes her as his lover.

As the autumn sun begins to lose its strength, so too does the aging God. He grows ever weaker as he lies next to the Goddess in the fading sun, even as he begins to grow stronger inside her womb, readying his return as the young God.

Samhain, October 31, marks the death of the elderly God, and is both the start and the end of the ancient calendar. The God's absence is only temporary, though, as he waits for his rebirth at Yule, to start the cycle of the seasons once again.

Many modern witches tend to focus solely on the Goddess and overlook the God, but you must realize that his presence is necessary to achieve balance. Even if you do not honor him on a daily basis, he can always be called on for help, especially for protection against negative influences, as it is his place to rule over the cities of man and over the burning wastelands and deserts.

past position: There was power in your life at one time, but you've neglected to maintain it. Somewhere along the way you surrendered that power to someone else, and that was a mistake. Think back to long ago and try to remember how it felt to be firmly in control of your own destiny, and you will see where you made your mistake.

present position: This symbol can be interpreted as power over others, strength of will, or political influence, but it should always be considered as a temporary condition. As with all things, the eventual decline is just around the corner.

future position: Prepare for bad times ahead. With a little careful preparation you may be able to minimize the worst of it. Go out of the way to make sure you've got enough essentials to last for a while, and you should be able to weather the coming storm without too much inconvenience.

Goddess

This symbol represents all three aspects of the Goddess—Maiden, Mother, and Crone.

The Maiden or youthful Goddess can be seen in the waxing crescent phase of the moon. She is often envisioned as a preteen girl, or sometimes as an adolescent. In this aspect she is filled with the promise of growth and new potential, and thus is usually associated with the spring planting season.

The full moon represents the Goddess as Mother, full of love and life. She is often depicted as pregnant at this time, full and round, much like the full moon itself. The new plants have begun to blossom, and animal life abounds. All of the Earth seems to be thriving under the protective influence of the Mother, and this is why this aspect is usually associated with the warmer growing season.

The waning crescent shows us the Goddess as Crone, filled with kindness and ancient wisdom. While the autumn winds grow ever colder, the earth seems to begin to yearn for the long slumber of winter. The ancient Goddess sitting close to a warm fire becomes the perfect symbol of the winter season.

The word "crone" has become associated with a negative image in modern times, but this has never been the case throughout history. A crone is simply an elderly witch, one who is to be revered and respected.

The Goddess is an equal partner with the God. Neither is beneath or above the other, but they represent two halves of a single coherent whole, lending balance to each other throughout the eternal cycle of the seasons.

She may lend us life for a brief period of time, but it always comes with the promise of death, as symbolized by the changing of the seasons. As with the seasons, eventual rebirth is the inevitable outcome as the cycle of birth, death, and rebirth continues uninterrupted.

past position: The innocence of youth runs hand in hand with foolish deeds. This stone will usually indicate a past error in judgment that resulted in someone being emotionally or physically harmed. Don't dwell on this and let one mistake ruin your life. You must get over this and continue living.

present position: Interpret the Goddess in a present position to mean either the start of a correct path, wisdom that is gained from another, or quite often both. Now is the time to keep your ears open and your mouth shut. Let what you hear from the people around you be your guide and take you in a new direction.

future position: If this stone appears in a future position, be sure to listen to other peoples' advice and try to gain their wisdom, but be skeptical of all they say. Someone will try to sidetrack you or give you false information, so check all of your facts carefully, and be absolutely sure you understand all of the ramifications of your actions before starting any new projects at this time.

Herbs

Virtually any plants, flowers, or leaves used in any form of magic can be called herbs. Some witches have kitchens filled with exotic spices from all over the world even though they don't cook.

Many pagans prefer to use fresh herbs as incense instead of store-bought cones or sticks, and burn the freshly ground herbs directly onto charcoal tablets that are available from most New Age stores. Many will use herbs to add into a ritual bath prior to spellcrafting, to mix with wine prior to ceremonies, or for a host of other ritual uses.

If you gather your own herbs, please follow these simple suggestions:

* Always gather them from as far from humanity as possible. This ensures their maximum purity.

* Gather only what you need, and never take so much from a single plant that it will not recover.

* Detach the leaves with your hands, instead of cutting them with scissors.

* Remember to always thank the plant for its sacrifice when you are finished.

To dry herbs for later use, simply hang a bundle by their stems for a few weeks and then crumble the leaves into a fine powder. You can also place them between two paper towels to dry faster, but this will leech some of the potency out of the herbs. Under no circumstances should you attempt to microwave herbs to dry them faster.

In general, the Goddess is honored by all watery and earthy flowers and seeds, white or purple blooms, and all sweet-scented herbs and flowers.

The God is honored by all fiery colored, airy, strongly scented herbs and flowers, or yellow and red blooms.

Entire volumes dedicated to the magical properties of herbs are available.

past position: In a past position, this stone will usually refer to a nice gesture that was rejected. This may be something special that you did for a loved one or for a stranger, but in either case you were rebuffed. Examine this past event carefully to see where you went wrong. Learn from your mistake, and then let it go.

present position: In a present position, read this stone as meaning a close tie to the earth, where balance and moderation are essential. Remember to maintain that balance in the very near future.

future position: In a future position, the Herb stone indicates that an offering will soon be needed, perhaps to placate someone or maybe just to be nice. Be careful not to miss this offering, as the opportunity it presents may never reveal itself again.

Magic circle

Magic circles can be traced as far back as ancient Babylon, and have been used by various traditions all over the globe throughout history. Middle Ages magicians in Europe believed that standing inside of the circle would protect them from the forces that they raised outside of the circle; however, most modern traditions now believe in just the opposite. Modern pagans use the circle to contain the magical energies that they raise from within themselves.

Also known as sacred space, the magic circle is a non-physical sphere of personal power that envelops the practitioner and contains the magical energies during rituals and spells. Some witches envision this sphere enveloping just themselves, while others extend it into the ground below. Either way seems to work just fine. It can be created by walking deosil around the altar, or by envisioning the sphere forming around you from your own energies.

The circle may be marked by a cord, a ring of flowers, a circle in the dirt, or by nothing at all. In the center of the circle is usually the altar, with the ritual tools laid out appropriately.

The north point of the circle belongs to the element of earth, and can be marked with salt, a stone, a clump of dirt, or symbolically by the pentacle. East belongs to air, and is usually marked by the censer or some other form of incense.

South is for fire, and is almost always marked with a candle. West is water, and should be marked by, naturally enough, a container of water such as the chalice.

Walking deosil around the altar is an ancient custom designed to define the perimeter of your magic circle and to raise energy within it. Many modern traditions will walk deosil several times to gather energy, then stop at the north point of the circle to invite the earth element to attend and be witness to their ceremony. The invitation is then extended to each element in turn after walking deosil again. Various invocations are used according to different traditions, but almost all agree that you should invite the elements into your circle, not command them to attend.

Once the elements have been invited, most traditions will then invite the Goddess and the God to attend in the same manner, and then whatever deities they wish to call upon. The circle is now complete, and your ritual may begin.

When finished, the circle is dispersed by walking widdershins to dispel any excess energies left over. The gods are usually thanked for attending, and each element is thanked in turn in the same manner that they were invited. The circle is now dispersed.

past position: This was a time when you demonstrated a lack of self-control in a situation that called for restraint. While you didn't know it at the time, it was a turning point in your life. Think back on how your life might have been different had your response been different.

present position: An opportunity to gain self-control and mastery over personal power is here. Look for the people in your life to point out the way to you, but they can not accompany you on the journey that lies ahead. This is a road you must travel alone for a short time if you wish to gain the benefits.

future position: Someone will try to gain mastery over you in the near future. It may arrive in the form of seduction, intimidation, negative energies, physical domination, or something else entirely, but it will come into your life in an appealing form, so be wary. Strive to achieve balance, and thus win over mastery.

Moon

The moon governs all of the life cycles of the Earth. As such, it is the perfect representation of the Goddess. Each phase of the moon's cycle can represent a different aspect of the Goddess.

The youthful Maiden can be seen as the waxing crescent, growing stronger and wiser with every day. The fertile Mother can be seen in the full moon, lending us unending energy and life. The Crone aspect can be seen as the waning crescent, starting her inevitable decline in strength.

New ventures should always be started under the waxing moon, for as the moon grows in strength, so will your ventures. This is also the classic time to start new spells.

Old ventures should always be concluded during the waning cycle, which makes this the perfect time for ending relationships, quitting smoking, etc.

New moons and full moons are special days of power, and should be used to advantage whenever possible. While there is no proof that spells cast on a full moon are any stronger than those cast at other times, the full moon can often seem to fill us with her power and lend us some of her energy, and thereby make the spellcaster stronger at this time. This does seem to have a very definite effect on the outcome of many types of spells.

Moon-cycle calendars are readily available, and this makes it simple for the modern witch to deliberately time spells so that they will start during the waxing phase and conclude during the waning phase of the moon, even if the spell itself lasts for many months.

past position: The moon symbol can be interpreted to mean creativity and adaptability, and may be referring to either a specific person or event in your past. In either case, it represents an end to a beginning, something that helped you to grow spiritually. Think back to a time when your imagination was fertile, and you will understand this stone.

present position: Interpret this as order existing within chaos. There is a decision you need to make at this time, and the outcome will cause change, either gradual or dramatic, and affect all those around you. Will you create the chaos or be the order within? The choice is yours.

future position: This is always a symbol of energy, but it may represent negative energy just as often as it represents positive, constructive energy. There will be someone trying to get close to you soon, and this person may already be in your life. Be sure this person has the type of energy you are looking for.

Moonrise

Symbolically, moonrise is seen as the time when the Goddess first chooses to become visible to us again, after keeping herself hidden from our sight since moonset. Now is when the moon seems to be closest to the Earth, actually appearing to touch the horizon as she returns to us once again. The energy radiating from the moon seems to be most abundant and easily tapped into at this time.

Moonrise rituals are common in many traditions, and many pagans insist that this is to honor the Goddess, whose symbol is the moon. Other authorities attribute this to the fact that using moonrise as a meeting time allowed common people to coordinate their actions secretly in societies where clocks were rare and expensive devices.

Spellcrafting at moonrise can often bring potent results. Rituals held and spells cast when sunset and moonrise nearly coincide are especially potent occasions for strong magic, as both the sun and the moon (the God and the Goddess) will be present to enhance your personal energy. This special opportunity to cast spells should never be missed.

The sight of the moon rising into the sky is meant to remind us of the Goddess, and we should always take a moment to honor her whenever we see the moon.

past position: You recently missed an excellent opportunity to gather and store personal energy that would have made things much easier for you now. You may not even have been aware of missing it when it happened, so keep your eyes open for new opportunities in the near future.

present position: There is an excellent opportunity to gather and store personal power available to you at this time. Take advantage of it. It will make things much easier for you in the near future if you do.

future position: An opportunity to draw on extra personal power is about to present itself to you unexpectedly, so look hard for it. It may come in a form that is very difficult to recognize. You will be glad that you took advantage of this shortly after, so keep your eyes open for it.

Moonset

Although she is always with us, the Goddess sometimes chooses to hide herself from our view. This does not mean she is abandoning us, but merely that there are times when we must depend on our own power to get us through the dark nights.

Traditionally, many pagan ceremonies started at moonrise and ended at moonset, but in modern times this can often be difficult to arrange due to tight, inflexible schedules forced on us by the industrialized society we live in.

When moonset and sunrise nearly coincide, this can be a perfect time for early morning spells, as the power of both the moon and the sun will be available for you to tap into.

Always take a moment to honor the Goddess whenever you see the moon in any of its phases, but when you glimpse a moonset take an extra moment to appreciate the Goddess before her absence is felt.

past position: This represents a time when you needed someone who wasn't there for you. You may have handled this situation poorly at the time, and your actions have cost you more than you may know.

present position: Now is the time to depend primarily on your own personal power and energies to get important things done. The deities may be testing you, or you may be testing yourself. Seek assistance from those around you, but do not force the issue with them.

future position: Be prepared to depend on your own personal power and energies in the very near future. There is a trial ahead of you—physical, mental, or spiritual—that you must face alone. You will be victorious if you prepare yourself now by gathering your energy.

New moon

This is the end of the moon's eternal cycle, but it is also its beginning. Each time it passes from our view, we are given the promise of renewal and continuity to come. This is a highly symbolic reminder of the belief in reincarnation that is held by virtually all traditions.

The new moon is used in some traditions to represent the time we humans spend between incarnations. Death is not seen as nonexistence, but merely as a time of waiting, much like the God waiting to be reborn between the death of the elderly God at Samhain and the birth of the youthful God at Yule. This, by the way, should in no way indicate that the new moon honors the God, as all phases of the moon are considered to be the domain of the Goddess by nearly every tradition.

Just as with the full moon, esbats (non-sabbat rituals) held on the new moon are especially potent, as this is also a night of great power. This is a time when the Goddess may choose to hide from our sight and our lives, and so is considered by many to be an excellent time to exercise your own personal powers and cast spells. It is well documented that the full moon can seem to fill us with strength and energy. Its complete absence from our view seems to do so as well.

Often new spells will be deliberately timed to end on the new moon, as this will lend finality and closure to those spells.

Spells to start new things (businesses, romances, etc.) should be started between the new moon and the full moon. As the moon grows stronger, so will your desired goal.

Spells to end or quit things (remove obsessions, quit smoking or drinking, etc.) should always be started between the full moon and the new moon. As the intensity of the moon shrinks, so will your problem.

past position: There is a new emptiness in your life that troubles you. Something has been removed from your daily life or is hidden from your view, and you miss it dearly. Don't worry, though. This is just a temporary condition.

present position: This should be interpreted as either a need for patience in daily situations, or as an excess of patience where it is not called for. Either way, things are not getting done as needed, and you need to change your own behavior in order for things to improve.

future position: Something that is important to you is soon to be hidden from your view. There is nothing you can do to avoid this, so the best thing to do is to remember that it's still there, even if you can't see it.

Pentacle

A pentacle is a wooden, clay, or metal disc inscribed with an interlaced five-pointed star and often with other, more obscure symbols. It is not to be confused with a pentagram, which is simply any five-sided object. For example, the Pentagon building in Washington, D.C., definitely qualifies as a pentagram, but certainly not as a pentacle.

The pentacle's use in ritual magic can be traced back well over 4,000 years, making this one of the oldest symbols in existence. Historically, they were often hung over doorways or windows as a protective device. In recent years, the pentacle has become associated with satanism and/or evil, mainly due to certain Hollywood movies, but this has never been the historical case. In fact, Native American shamans have used this symbol on their medicine shields for many centuries to bring dreams, healing, and protection.

The five-pointed star is symbolic of humanity ruling wisely over the four elements of nature—earth, air, fire, and water. The enclosing circle has been described either historically as the encompassing power of the deities, or alternately in modern times as the Earth itself.

In quite a few rituals, the pentacle is used with other tools on the altar to represent the four elements. While traditions vary widely, a common practice is to lay out the altar with the pentacle to the north to represent earth, the wand to the south to represent air, the athame to the east to represent fire, and the chalice to the west to represent water.

Some traditions use the pentacle to either attract or repel energies, based on how the pentacle was created. A pentacle drawn starting with a line from the top point of the star to the bottom left point first (making the final line from the bottom right point to the top) is believed to invoke energy. Drawing it in the reverse fashion is often believed to dispel the same energies, though there are differing opinions on exactly what to reverse (the order in which the lines are drawn, the direction of each line, the starting point, etc.).

past position: This indicates a time in your life when there was a lack of resistance on your part that may not have been beneficial to you. There was something that you were meant to do, but you complied with others' wishes instead. Don't worry and be patient. The opportunity will eventually present itself again.

present position: Interpret this stone to mean harmony in life and balance in all things. You may have already created this for yourself, or you may be striving for it. In either case, there is work ahead if you still want that balance to be in your life.

future position: The pentacle usually indicates calm waters and smooth sailing ahead, but be sure to stay on the lookout. Be aware of the sudden storms coming over the horizon and you should be able to outmaneuver them without a problem.

Rebirth

Reincarnation is one of the oldest religious concepts, believed to have existed even in prehistory. Anthropologists theorize that soon after animism ("I am a reasoning being, therefore that tree must also be"), the human race developed the concept of a never-ending cycle of birth, death, and rebirth that is evidenced all around us in nature. This is illustrated most clearly in the eternal cycle of the seasons. It is the birth of abundant new life in the spring, the bountiful growth of the summer, the gradual decline of the autumn, the slumbering death of the winter, followed once again by the rebirth of life in the spring.

In most modern pagan traditions, the God serves as the perfect example of this eternal cycle. He grows in the womb of the Goddess during the late winter, waiting quietly like the dormant plants to be reborn with the spring. Summer sees him strong and able, lusting after his eternal mate, the Goddess. They couple and spread their fertility to all the crops and animals of the land and sea. The fall harvest sees the God begin his inevitable decline, much like the sun's warming rays that are growing weaker daily. The death of the God on Samhain (October 31) heralds the coming of winter, and is one of the most important dates on any tradition's calendar. Even as the God is dying, he knows that he is also growing ever stronger inside the womb of his Goddess.

Winter brings dormancy, but also the promise that spring and the God's rebirth will always be right around the corner year after year.

It is in the certainty of death that accompanies every life—and the promise of life that accompanies every death—that the eternal cycle shows itself to us. It is all of creation held in perpetually changing balance.

past position: Rebirth in the past position represents a time when conflict was abundant in your life, but you still managed to prevail. Reflect on this time to gain special insights.

present position: Your life is currently in balance, but far from free of conflicting forces. You've managed to achieve an uneasy stalemate with yourself, but it won't last for very long. Now is the time to make a choice.

future position: It is more important than ever to maintain the level of balance you've managed to achieve in your life, or else the scales may rock to one side forcefully enough to dislodge you. Be prepared for unexpected news, or the message might tip the scales for you.

Salt

Salt is believed by most pagans to have the ability to absorb negative energy. Since this type of psychic residue accumulates wherever people gather, indoor rituals and spells usually require purifying the area prior to starting any strong magic, and this can be done by scattering salt, either alone or mixed with herbs. A besom is then used to ritually sweep the area clean, even though the actual bristles need never touch the ground. This method is used in many cleansing rituals in many different cultures.

Salt is most commonly believed to be linked to the element of earth. Sea salts are preferred by many because of the close association between the Goddess and the sea, though it is common to find rock salt, Epsom salt, or even table salt used instead.

Bath salts are quite common and easily obtained at any drugstore, and many witches will purify themselves prior to starting rituals and spells with a ritual bath. Store-bought bath salts are fine, but some witches prefer to make their own, believing that if they create the bath salts with a specific purpose in mind, they will be more effective. If a few drops of an essential oil are added into the water to represent the element of fire, and incense is burned during the bath to represent air, all four elements will be gathered together to assist you.

Salt may also be consecrated for ritual use, although many believe that this is redundant, as salt is a natural negative energy absorber, and therefore "pre-consecrated," if you will. Some witches will use salt instead of a cord in casting a magic circle. As with all such things, whatever works best for you is what you should do.

past position: This represents something that needed to be purified, but continued on in your life without cleansing. It can quite often refer to another person or to an incident involving another person, but it may also be a shared thing between you and another. You know that this has been in your life too long, and you will not be able to grow spiritually until you have performed this cleansing, so take care of this as soon as possible.

present position: The salt symbol almost always indicates a need for cleansing or purifying, but it can often refer to someone else in your life, and not to you. Make sure you understand this need, as it may be that you need to clean this person out of your life if he or she will not clean up their own act.

future position: Something or someone is about to rain negative energy into your life, so be on your guard. You can avoid this if you see it coming, but beware of what appears to be the easy path, as this will lead to even worse events.

Spring

The modern pagan calendar notes February 2 as the sabbat of Imbolc. It has traditionally been known by other names as well, including Oimelc, Brigid's Day, the Feast of Torches, and many others.

The Goddess has recovered after giving birth to the infant God on Yule, and begins to stir and wake from her slumber. She covers all the Earth with her blessings as the young God stretches and grows stronger, and the days slowly become longer. His energy warms the fertile earth and causes new seeds to sprout, heralding the return of spring.

Ancient Europeans celebrated this day with torches and huge balefires to honor the return of the sun's (the God's) strength. A woman wearing a wreath of candles on her head is associated with this day in many cultures, and it is one of the few images from our ancient pagan heritage that has been handed down to us without some sort of negative association having been added. For obvious reasons, most modern women now choose to carry a candle in their ceremonies rather than risk catching fire.

Modern pagans will often use this occasion to perform purification rituals after the long, shut-in months of the winter, purging their homes of accumulated psychic residue.

This is also seen by most as the proper time for initiations into covens, or to perform self-dedication rituals by solo practitioners.

Near the end of March, the length of the day and the night are equally balanced. This is the spring equinox, and marks the sabbat of Ostara, also sometimes called Eostra's Day. The exact date will change from year to year, since our current calendar is not based on the solar cycles but on the sidereal year, which marks the movement of the stars' positions through their journey across the sky.

The Goddess is now fully awake after her long winter slumber, and the young God is quickly maturing into his adult aspect. They walk through the fields, causing fertility and abundance wherever they pass. Natural energies can be felt stirring, about to be spurred into a frenzy of spring activity and new growth. The spring equinox is a time of new beginnings and action, so plant spells that will blossom into future gains at this time.

This sabbat should not be confused in any way with the modern holiday of Easter, although it is interesting to note that the Christian church uses the spring equinox to calculate the date of their holiday. Easter always falls on the first Sunday following the first full moon following the spring equinox. Many have marveled at the fact that the church uses what seems to be a very pagan method to calculate one of their most holy days.

past position: This represents a specific event in your past, one that signified that a time for new beginnings was now over. It may have been monumental or almost unnoticed, but you knew the incident when it occurred. The doors that closed then may reopen soon.

present position: A time of new beginnings is just starting for you. Be creative and unafraid as you embark on your new journeys, but always remain the cautious traveler when you are in unfamiliar territory.

future position: A time of new beginnings will soon occur, although it may disguise itself as something different. Peel away the mask and examine the face beneath before you make any decisions or take any actions.

Summer

The first of the summer celebrations is the sabbat of Beltane, sometimes called May Day, on April 30, which marks the passage of the young God into his full adult power. He pursues and wins the heart of the Goddess, and she takes him as her lover. They fall in love, and the God impregnates the Goddess.

The Goddess and the God seem to radiate power, health, and energy after their coupling, and this spreads to all the plants and animals of the world and brings forth abundant new life.

The classic maypole is a direct descendant from ancient Beltane fertility celebrations. For those who have never seen a real maypole, it is simply a tall wooden pole (an obviously phallic symbol) with ribbons or strings attached to the top. Participants form a circle around the pole, and each one takes a string. Every other person then turns to face his or her left, and the remaining people turn to face to their right. The two groups then move forward, passing each other first to the right, then to the left, then to the right, etc., inter-twining the strings as they wrap around the pole, often to the accompanying rhythm of a drum.

In some modern traditions it is still used to generate fertil-ity energy, and a couple that is unsuccessful at having a child may sit together at the base of the maypole while a group generates and focuses energy toward their desired goal.

The sabbat of Midsummer, sometimes called Litha, is a celebration of abundance on the summer solstice, the longest day of the year near the end of June. Like all solstices and equinoxes, the exact date changes from year to year due to our calendar.

This is the day when the powers of nature are at their peak, as the God and Goddess luxuriate in the lush greenery and abundant wildlife, and so is considered by many to be the classic time for magic of all types.

Balefires were important to the ancients on this day, and the practice of leaping a balefire to bring prosperity, health, and good fortune continues to be a common practice on this sabbat. Some traditions believe that couples who are still unsuccessful at producing offspring can gain special fertility by leaping the balefire hand in hand.

past position: You have missed an opportunity for powerful magic. The expenditure of a small amount of energy would have resulted in huge gains, had you taken action long ago. You may be about to repeat this mistake.

present position: There is a need for powerful magic in your life right now. It may be needed to build something new, to reinforce something already existing, or to tear down something that has outlived its usefulness. Use the potential that you have to its fullest.

future position: You will soon have a need for powerful magic in your life. There will be no tragedy if this need goes unfulfilled, but it will make things much easier in the long run if you use all of your knowledge to prepare for the times ahead now, and take action only when the time is right.

Sun

The sun is the symbol of the God, just as the moon is the symbol of the Goddess. It is the provider of warmth and light as it shines down upon us during the day, just as the youthful God radiates energy to all those around him. Just as the moon governs all the cycles of the Earth, the sun guides the seasons through their eternal cycles.

Celebrations to the sun, such as the summer and winter solstices (the longest and shortest days of the year) and the spring and autumn equinoxes (when the days are of equal length as the nights), should be started either at dawn or at noon, when the sun is most powerful. They should end at sunset, when the sun gives dominion over to the moon. These four solar festivals of the witch's calendar (Yule, Ostara, Litha, and Mabon) celebrate the yearly cycles of planting, growth, harvest, and rebirth.

Yule is a celebration of the rebirth of the young God on the winter solstice, the shortest day of the year. The newborn baby is weak, as is the sun's strength, but both will begin growing stronger rapidly.

Imbolc (February 22) honors the youthful God as he stretches and grows stronger daily, like the returning sun. His energy warms the fertile earth and causes new seeds to sprout. The lengthening of the daylight hours coincides with the growth of the God's strength. Ostara is celebrated on the spring equinox, as the God is quickly growing into his adult aspect. He pursues the Goddess, and they fall in love.

Beltane (April 30) marks the passage of the young God into his full adult power, as he takes the Goddess as his lover. This is the classic time for fertility rituals of all types. The summer solstice, or Litha, marks the height of both the God's power and the sun's strength, as this is the longest day of the year.

Lughnasadh (August 1) marks the first harvest, as the sun and the God both begin to lose their strength. Their rapid decline is inevitable, and both will grow ever weaker until the celebration of Mabon on the autumn equinox, after which the days will begin to be shorter than the nights. This decline continues, resulting in the death of the elderly God on Samhain (October 31). The daylight hours continue to become shorter and colder until Yule is reached once again, and the eternal cycle continues uninterrupted.

The stars, as distant suns, fall into the God's domain.

past position: Interpret this stone as a major source of psychic energy or personal power. This may be a person or even a belief that you drew strength from or were inspired by at one time. Rarely will this source of power still be in your life, but it is even rarer that it has been replaced with a new source just as strong. You may have searched for a replacement in vain, but you gave up too soon.

present position: Now is the time to tap into your unused energy. There is something that you need to do, but you don't believe that you are up to the task. You will do fine when the time comes, but first you will need to tap into the vast amounts of energy all around you in order to be ready. Now is a perfect time to cast spells for strength.

future position: There will be a major source of energy and personal power to be gained soon. It may come in the form of something already in your life, something within yourself, or something from another person. Be careful not to miss this opportunity when it comes, or it won't present itself again without causing you to expend a serious amount of your own energy next time.

Sunrise

The God is entering into his domain and banishing the night from the skies. He rises each day and renews the cycle of light and dark that governs all of our days. In ascension, he is gaining in strength even though he knows that the onset of night is inevitable. The energy he gives to the world can be felt in the warmth of his light.

For practical purposes (as well as to add an air of mystery), most ceremonies and rites were historically held at night. This is attributed mainly to the need for secrecy during the Burning Times, when anonymity was a matter of life and death. However the equinoxes and solstices (Yule, Ostara, Midsummer, and Mabon) are solar rituals, and should more naturally be held at noon or dawn whenever possible and practical.

Sunrise on the summer solstice is a special time of power, and it is clear that many ancient cultures understood this. In fact, the ancient entrance pathway to Stonehenge in southern England is aligned perfectly with the position of the sun at sunrise on the longest day of the year, the summer solstice. It is also interesting to note that the exit pathway is perfectly aligned with the sunset on the shortest day of the year, the winter solstice, exactly 180 degrees away on the horizon.

past position: This represents a nexus, an event that influenced the outcome of the rest of your life. Status and power were down one path, and mediocrity down the other. You may not even have been aware when you chose your path, but now is the time to remember and reexamine that event.

present position: You are ready for a rise in status, position, or power, so seize the opportunity that's in front of you. Be careful to acknowledge the efforts of the people around you or the rise will quickly change into a fall.

future position: Get ready for something special in your life. There is a huge gain to be made soon, but you will have to be very aware of those around you if you want to take advantage of this opportunity. Make an effort to meet someone new and you will gain special insight as well.

Sunset

This symbol is often associated with Lughnasadh or Mabon, the autumn sabbats. The sun itself is seen by virtually all traditions as a symbol of the God, so sunset can be seen as symbolic of the elderly God's time of failing strength. He knows that time is almost up, but he also knows that he will return as part of the never-ending cycle, just as the spring must follow the winter and the sun must return every morning. This is highly symbolic of the almost universal belief in reincarnation that most traditions hold.

Sunset is the classic time for the start of most rituals. Some witches believe this is can be attributed solely to the need for anonymity and secrecy, and are quick to point out clearly documented instances throughout history where witches, pagans, and even atheists have needed to remain secret in order to safeguard their own lives. Other traditions believe that the reason most rituals start at sundown is to honor the Goddess, whose symbol is the moon.

Most witches will admit that holding a night ritual by balefire under the cover of darkness adds an air of mystery and intrigue that can heighten the atmosphere and mood of a gathering, and thus make the magic they do more potent. Most will also admit that the need to fear for their lives, if discovered, is mainly a thing of the past. It is unfortunate in this enlightened age that there are still numerous cases of religious persecution being committed against pagans every day, and people can still lose their jobs, homes, and much more for believing in one of the most ancient traditions.

Even though most rituals have historically been held at night, many modern practitioners believe that solar celebrations, the solstices and the equinoxes, should properly be held during the day, and timed to start at sunrise and/or end at sunset whenever possible. Many practitioners will deliberately do this to give honor to the God.

past position: A past betrayal has been holding you back. You recently missed an opportunity because of your hesitation to extend trust. Learn from your mistake. Don't automatically distrust everyone else because of it.

present position: This usually indicates a lessening in status, position, or power, and it may be someone who you thought you could trust who is responsible for this decline. Look closely.

future position: Prepare yourself, for deception is about to happen. A chain of events is already in motion that will lead to this, but you can avoid the worst of it if you take steps to head it off now. Regardless of the steps you may take, some damage has already occurred. Be careful how you proceed from here.

Wand

Recognized by all as the symbol of kings and dignitaries, the wand has, over the centuries, become associated with wisdom and spiritual maturity. The use of a wand in ritual magic can be traced as far back as the ancient Celts, but it is believed that its use predates any recorded history, so it is believed by many to be the oldest tool.

The wand is a tool of invocation, and is often used to call upon the Goddess and the God or other specific deities during rituals. Never used for commanding, the wand is used to invite the deities, and sometimes the four elements, to enter your magic circle and witness your ritual.

This tool can also be used to direct personal energy, to draw magic circles or symbols on the ground or in the air, or to represent the element of air. Placing a crystal or other precious stone at the tip of the wand has become common practice, and it is believed to help direct the flow of personal energy toward its intended purpose.

Wands made of wood are traditional, and rowan wood was thought to make the best wands by the Celts, but other woods, such as willow, oak, or apple, have come into common use. Many believe that a wooden wand is needed to offset and balance the metal athame; however, wands made entirely of crystal have also become fashionable in recent years.

Copper wands are sometimes used, as copper is believed by many to be an excellent conductor of psychic energy, and it is a simple matter to affix a crystal onto the end of a hollow copper tube. Since copper is a relatively soft metal, etching mystical symbols onto a copper wand is also very easy.

Wands may have incredibly ornate carvings, leather bindings, crystals, beads, gemstones, or other decorations attached, or may be as simple as a twig found lying on the ground.

Some traditions believe that the proper size for a wand should be one cubit, or the distance from the point of your elbow to the tip of your middle finger. Other traditions prefer the use of a ritual staff instead of a wand. While both have their appeals, the wand is much easier to wield and takes up much less storage space.

past position: Often in this position the wand can indicate a time when you squandered your personal energy and wasted it on frivolous pursuits. You must learn from your old mistakes, but you must also learn to then let them go. You may need to stop dwelling on the past and start thinking about the future instead.

present position: Interpret the wand as an immediate need to focus and direct your own personal energy. Now is the time when you need to find the focus that you lack, and then to redirect all of your energies toward that focus. Take a good look around yourself and carefully examine what you believe to be true about yourself, and you will find what you need.

future position: The time is soon coming when you will find an unexpected new direction in your life, so be ready when it happens and you won't be overwhelmed. Change is inevitable, but just remember that the nature of the universe is cyclical, and that eventually all things return to where they started.

Waning moon

This is the classic time of endings. Spells to quit things (stop smoking, dispel disease, end relationships, etc.) should always be started under the waning moon. Older spells or other ventures should also be ended during this phase whenever possible.

The waning moon is often seen as a symbolic representation of the Goddess in her Crone aspect—the ancient source of all wisdom, comfort, and knowledge. The elderly crone is closely linked to prophecy and strong magic in most traditions, so it is believed by many witches that divination is especially effective during this moon phase. This is often the time that witches and pagans receive sudden insights, and answers to questions that they didn't even know to ask.

Meditation and quiet contemplation are recommended during this phase, and will almost always result in some unexpected revelation.

As with the waxing moon, there are no specific rituals to honor the waning moon; however, many of the autumn rites could be easily adapted to this moon phase. Any rite dedicated to the Goddess as Crone is also appropriate.

Just as an aside, the word "crone" has become associated with a negative image in modern times—namely the ugly, green, wart-nosed, broom-riding, child-stealing Halloween character. This has never been the historic case, as the title of crone has always been a coveted position, and quite simply means an elderly witch. A crone is someone who is to be revered and cherished for her wisdom, power, and knowledge, not someone to be shunned and outcast.

past position: This is something that you should have quit or ended long ago. It no longer brings happiness into your life, and you really should eliminate it as soon as you are strong enough to part with it.

present position: Sudden insight is possible now. Carefully examine what is happening in your life. Meditation and contemplation may not change your current circumstances, but will result in a sudden insight that has been eluding you for some time now.

future position: This stone indicates a time of peaceful, natural endings is about to enter your life, or it may also mean the end of something yet to come.

Water

This is one of the four prime elements that give energy to all things—earth, air, fire, and water. Water is a cleansing element, so water spells naturally include those for love, purity, and psychic works, and many traditions link the besom, or broom, to the element of water because of its cleansing properties.

Water is also one of the most versatile magical ingredients. It can be bathed in, drunk, sprinkled, or used to anoint new initiates. There are, in fact, very few spells that do not use water in one way or another, either as an ingredient or as an element to be honored.

Most traditions still hold that spells and rituals require some form of symbolic cleansing prior to starting, both for the area it's to be held in and for the practitioner. Ritual baths involving salts, oils, and herbs are a common practice among most witches prior to performing strong magic of any sort. A bath will also relax and clarify the thoughts of the practitioner by temporarily isolating them from most daily distractions, allowing the caster to focus on the coming ritual or spell.

The chalice filled with water is usually placed on the left side of the altar to honor the Goddess. The cauldron may be filled with water for many different magical purposes. A cup or bowl of water can also be placed on the west compass point in a magic circle to represent the element of water.

Emotions, psychic power, healing, beauty, love, and spirituality all belong to the realm of the water element, so most spells that address these issues will heavily rely on water magic, or at least involve water as a prime ingredient.

past position: Water is always a symbol of cleansing or purity, but in the past position it refers to the well-being of the mind. It may be that there was something in your past that has caused you to neglect some part of your development as a person. This event relates directly to the rest of your reading.

present position: In this position, water refers to emotional well-being or love. There is a significant change in your life right now that is soon to affect your well-being, for good or bane. It's not too late to stop this change from occurring, but should you? You already know the answer.

future position: In the future position, water will refer to spirituality. There is a test of your faith looming over the horizon, but it is not too late for you to avoid it. If you do, you may need to renew your faith soon, or risk losing it altogether.

Waxing moon

"Waxing" is simply an old word for "growing," and almost all witches see the waxing moon, as the moon grows from the hidden new moon into its first quarter crescent, as the time of new beginnings.

New ventures and spells to bring things into your life (such as love, wealth, health, etc.) should always be started during this phase of the moon, as the symbolism of the growing moon will add strength to your spells.

The waxing moon is viewed in most traditions as being symbolic of the Maiden Goddess, represented as a preteen girl or sometimes as a young child, still innocent of the world around her yet growing wiser, stronger, and smarter on a daily basis. As her strength grows, so does her knowledge and power until she enters the Goddess as Mother aspect with the full moon.

Just as spring must give way to summer over and over again, the waxing moon only has a limited time until it must inevitably change into the next aspect.

Most traditions have no special gathering at this time, and while there are very few specific rituals that are designed to be held at the first quarter waxing moon, many spring rituals could be easily modified to fit this moon phase if you are so inclined. This is believed by most practitioners to be a classic time for new magic.

past position: A part of you views the past as a time when things were full of unrecognized potential, but as in all things magical you must remember that the cycles of life never really end. Highs are always followed by lows, and vice versa, and the next wave is always just around the corner.

present position: The waxing moon in this position can be interpreted as the start of a new relationship, business, adventure, etc., so now is the time to take a chance and do more than just dream.

future position: Things will be improving greatly soon. The waxing moon is in your future and both spiritual and physical gains are just ahead. Look sharp, or you may miss them when they present themselves.

Widdershins

The practice of walking widdershins, or counterclockwise, around the altar can be traced back to ancient Europeans who reverenced the sun.

In most modern traditions, walking widdershins—against the sun's apparent motion through the sky—is used to disperse negative energy or unwanted conditions such as disease or mental imbalance, or to disperse a magic circle after rituals are finished.

Some pagan traditions believe that you can raise negative energy by circling the altar widdershins. This is not a common practice because the vast majority of modern witches shun dealing with negative energy in any form, believing that the energy they put out will return to them threefold. This is known as the Rule of Three or the Threefold Law by most traditions, and was best stated by Scott Cunningham in his book *Wicca: A Guide for the Solitary Practitioner* as follows:

"Ever mind the Rule of Three.
Three times what thou givest returns to thee.
This lesson well, thou must learn.
Thee only gets what thou dost earn!"

It is interesting to note that at the end of some Catholic funerals, the priest will circle the coffin three times widdershins while swinging the censer. It is believed by many that this was originally an ancient pagan custom intended to disperse any residual personal energy left in the corpse, while the rising smoke from the censer aided the spirit in its journey to the gods. Many such examples of purely pagan behavior can be found in virtually all forms of organized religions today.

If you are in the Southern Hemisphere, switch the meaning of widdershins with deosil, as the apparent motion of the sun through the sky is reversed there.

past position: This represents a time when you made a bad decision and you knew it, but you went ahead and did it anyway. You ignored the voice of reason and threw caution to the wind, and you paid for it. Be careful not to repeat this pattern in the near future.

present position: You have already started down an incorrect path, or you've already made a very bad decision. It's too late to avoid all of the consequences, but you can minimize the damage if you face up to your mistake and take action to correct it right now.

future position: This is usually a bad decision or the start of an incorrect path, but one that still lies in the future. It's not too late to avoid this mistake if you reconsider your actions and decisions right now. Waiting for a sudden insight may cause you to be too late to do anything except watch as the damage occurs.

Wine

Often a chalice filled with wine and herbs will be shared during rituals, passed from person to person around the circle to symbolically join the group together. This ancient practice is still demonstrated in various forms in many modern religions.

After dispersing the sacred space left over from a ritual or spell, it is traditional in many covens for all to drink a small amount of wine or juice and to eat a small biscuit or piece of bread. This practice is known as the "simple feast" or sometimes as "cakes and ale." As products of the earth, the drink and food are meant to remind us of the part of us that is physical in nature, and to bring us down from the emotional and spiritual high that many celebrants experience after shared rituals. It is also said by some to ground excess energies left unused after your crafting is finished, much like walking widdershins to disperse a magic circle.

This is also a perfect time for socializing if you are part of a coven or other pagan group. Celebrants often use this time as an opportunity to chat about events in their daily lives, to greet friends they haven't seen in a while, and to get to know any new members better. While the magical uses of this practice have been stripped away or forgotten by most modern religions, the tradition of a "coffee and donut" hour after most services lives on, even if just for the social reasons.

There is a relatively modern twist to this tradition, in that some witches and/or covens specify that alcoholic beverages of any kind must not be allowed in their circles under any circumstance, and will substitute some sort of fruit juice on all occasions that call for wine. Other pagan groups seem to embrace alcohol and revel in their own self-induced euphoria at every opportunity. These two examples are the extremes, of course, and do not reflect the average pagan. Again, there are no set rules to follow regarding alcohol consumption, except for whatever seems right in your own life. Remember that balance and moderation should be sought in all things, and that includes how much and how often you imbibe.

past position: This represents a time when your primary emphasis was on the physical nature of the universe, and you thought less about the spiritual. This was not a bad thing at the time, but as children grow into adults, so must our physical nature grow into balance with our spiritual nature.

present position: Now is the time for emphasizing the physical nature of the universe over the spiritual. Meet with friends and rejoice in their companionship. This is the perfect time for a vacation or to take a trip you've wanted to go on. Enjoy yourself!

future position: Soon a time will come to seek emphasis of the physical over the spiritual. This does not say to abandon your spirituality, just to tip the scales slightly in the other direction. This will help you to balance them again later on.

Winter

The first of the winter sabbats is Samhain, the Feast of the Dead, or Allhallows Eve, universally celebrated on October 31. This day marks both the end and the beginning of the pagan calendar, and commemorates the death of the elderly God. His absence is just temporary, though, as he readies himself to be born again of the Goddess. This is a time for quiet reflection on the past year for most modern pagans.

This night is also considered by most traditions to be the time when the veil between the living and the dead is the thinnest. Many traditions will honor and remember their lost ones with the Wild Hunt or a similar ceremony, during which a doorway or archway will be specified as belonging to the dead. Any departed souls who would visit (without causing harm) are invited to enter back into the world and spend time with the living for a short while.

Many misconceptions have surrounded this ancient practice, and it is believed by many to be the origin of the modern holiday of Halloween, where otherwise normal non-pagan people dress up as horrible figures in an attempt to scare the pagan dead back into their resting places.

The winter solstice, the longest night and the shortest day of the year, marks the sabbat of Yule near the end of December. Just like the sabbat of Ostara, this celebration should in no way be confused or associated with Christian holidays that came much later in history.

Yule commemorates the rebirth of the infant God. The Goddess is exhausted from her labor, and sleeps in the winter desolation. Just as the sun (the God's symbol) will slowly gain strength in the lengthening days to come, so, too, will the young God gain power, until he is once again the mighty lover of the Goddess.

The eternal story of the Goddess and the God is symbolic, of course, and should not be interpreted as incest in any form. The coupling of the Goddess and the God was meant to express complex concepts by simple people, such as the eternal nature of life and the never-ending cycle of the seasons that was evidenced all around them. The story of the Goddess and the God is meant as just another reminder to us all that the ultimate result of death is simply rebirth.

past position: This stands for a misunderstood event in your past. While it was seen as an ending at the time, it later turned out to be a new beginning instead. This event has special bearing on the rest of your reading.

present position: The time for new beginnings is at hand. It may seem like you are in the dead of winter, but with a tiny bit of effort you can turn it into spring.

future position: The time for new beginnings will soon be approaching. What you do now will determine how smoothly this future beginning will go, so be especially aware of the effects you have on other people around you. Prepare yourself and be ready when it happens.

Simple Spells

Banishing negative influences

This spell may be performed at any time; however, its effectiveness will be enhanced if performed between a full moon and the following new moon.

Required stones:

* Goddess
* God
* Water
* Wand
* Censer
* Widdershins

* Bane
* Salt
* Athame
* Candle
* Wine

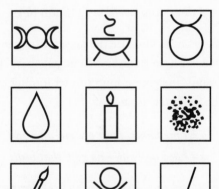

Prepare your layout space. When you have completed this, begin by placing the Candle stone in the center of your altar space. As you do so, say:

A candle's light to give true sight.

Next place the Water and Salt stones to either side of the Candle stone. As you do so, say:

With water, with salt, with purity's might.

Now place the Goddess, Censer, and God stones in their appropriate places. As you do so, say:

My Goddess, my God, and the spirit of air—
Hearken ye all! Thou art just and fair!

Place the Wand and Athame stones in their places. As you do so, say:

With wand and athame,
I direct and wield my will this day.

Take a moment to visualize the negative influence in your life that you wish to banish. When you have the image firmly in mind, imagine a long tunnel leading away from you into the far distance, and say:

To all my banes, both present and past,
you have no hold—no grip that lasts!

Now picture all the negative influences fleeing down the tunnel. Hold this image as long as possible. When you can no longer hold the images in your mind, place the Bane stone in its proper place, and say:

Banes take flight, banes vanish from sight.
There are no banes to trouble my life.

Now remove all of the stones except the Candle.

Place the Widdershins stone to the left of the Candle stone, and the Wine stone to the right of the Candle stone. The Widdershins stone is used to disperse any extraneous energy and the Wine stone is used to ground it. Take a few moments to thank the deities for their assistance and benevolence, then remove the Candle, Wine, and Widdershins stones in that order and put them away.

For clarity of thought

This spell may be performed indoors or outdoors, at any time of the year, during any phase of the moon.

Required stones:

- ★ Salt
- ★ Candle
- ★ Bane
- ★ Sun
- ★ Censer
- ★ Water
- ★ Widdershins
- ★ Moon

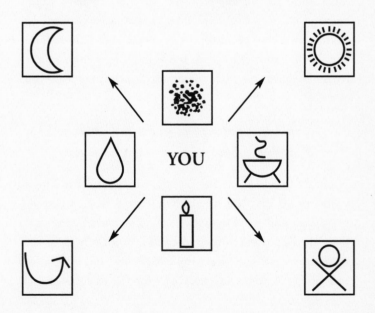

Select a suitable location where you will not be disturbed. It should be somewhere that you are comfortable, somewhere that is quiet, and above all else it should be somewhere that you will not be disturbed for the length of the spell. Once you are satisfied with your location, prepare your layout space.

Kneel or sit in the center of your circle, facing north. Place the Salt stone in front of you, the Censer stone to the right, the Candle stone behind you, and the Water stone to the left. Visualize the power of the four elements flooding into your circle, and say:

Elements of fire, earth, water, and air
Bring forth your powers, your energies' share.

Hold the Bane stone in your right hand and the Widdershins stone in your left. Visualize the Bane stone as representing confusion and the Widdershins stone as representing distraction. Place the Bane stone to the right and behind you, at the same time, place the Widdershins stone to the left and behind you. Slide the stones directly away from you as you say:

Confusions, distractions, within and without,
I put them behind me, no shadows, no doubts.

Hold the Sun stone in your right hand and the Moon stone in your left. Visualize the Sun stone as representing organization and the Moon stone as representing creativity. Place the Sun stone to the right and in front of you; at the same time, place the Moon stone to the left and in front of you. Slide the stones directly away from you as you say:

Order, creation, without and within,
I move them before me, to my life now come in.

Remove all of the witching stones, put them away, and then dismiss your sacred space.

For strength of spirit

Perform outdoors, preferably on a sunny day

This spell can be performed on any sunny summer day. However, if your casting is performed on the day of the summer solstice, it will have added strength and effectiveness.

Required stones:

- ★ Altar
- ★ Athame
- ★ Summer
- ★ Sunrise
- ★ Wand
- ★ Sun
- ★ God
- ★ Sunset

Select a suitable location. It should be a quiet place, out-doors, where you can see the sun rise and set. It also should be a place where your layout will not be disturbed. Begin just before sunrise by facing west, and prepare your layout space.

Place the Altar stone first. Put it in the center position closest to you. As you place the stone, say:

Altar symbol, oak for strength.

Next place the Summer stone above and to the left of the Altar stone. As you place the stone, say:

Midsummer, solstice, day's longest length.

Above the Summer stone place the Wand stone. As you place the stone, say:

This wand, this tool, to invoke.

Now place the God stone across from the Wand stone, as shown in the diagram. As you do this, say:

The God I beseech, strength be my cloak.

Beneath the God stone place the Athame stone to com-plete the circle, and say:

My athame I set now.
Complete my altar,
your strength endow.

As the sun rises, speak the following incantation and place the Sunrise stone in its place above the Altar:

O rising sun, symbol of the God,
let your strength flow into my heart
as your light flows into the day.

Take a moment to appreciate the sunrise. Thank the God for his assistance and take one step back from the layout. Now go about your day. Return as the sun reaches its highest point in the sky.

Before stepping up to your layout, take a moment or two to meditate and return your mind to the proper state of awareness. When you feel you are ready, take the one step up to your layout. Pick up and place the Sun stone above the Sunrise stone and speak the following incantation:

O sun on high, shining symbol of the God,
your strength fills my heart as your light fills the day.

Take a moment to appreciate the warmth of the midday sunlight and all that it reveals around you. Thank the God for his assistance and take one step back from the layout. Now go about the rest of your day. Return at sunset.

Before stepping up to your layout, take a moment or two to meditate and return your mind, once again, to the proper state of awareness. When you feel you are ready, take the one step up to your layout. As the first rim of the sun dips below the horizon, pick up and place the Sunset stone above the Sun stone, completing the pattern of the layout. Now speak the following words:

O setting sun, symbol of the God,
your strength fills my heart though your light may recede.
Your strength I retain, renewed with every dawn.

Meditate while you appreciate the setting of the sun. As the last rays of the sun fade from the sky, thank the God for his assistance and remove all of the stones. Put them away and dismiss your sacred space.

Achieving balance & equilibrium

Perform whenever necessary

The first time this spell is cast should be under a waning moon and then again under each of the next three moon phases.

Required stones:

- Full Moon
- Waxing Moon
- Winter
- Summer
- Athame
- Deosil

- New Moon
- Waning Moon
- Spring
- Autumn
- Wand
- Widdershins

Create your magic circle. Seat yourself comfortably in the center and prepare the area around you for your layout. Take a moment to compose your mind and concentrate on the ritual you are about to perform. The stones are to be laid out to form three circles around the caster (you). Each circle has four stones to anchor it. Speak each line of the following Words of Balance one at a time. After speaking each line, place the appropriate stone, as indicated, into its position, as shown in the table on page 115.

When you have reached the end of the Words of Balance, all of the stones should be in their proper alignments and you should be seated comfortably again. Sit quietly a moment within the circles you've created and then repeat the Words of Balance, only this time remove the appropriate stones from the layout. When all of the stones have been removed you may either start over (perform as many repetitions as you wish) or you may put the stones away and disperse your circle.

Words of Balance	Corresponding Stone	Placement Circle
New beginnings make endings	Full Moon	**outer circle:** Represents the boundary between chaos and order and the cycles of life that we are all a part of.
From endings, begin	New Moon	
From children to elders	Waxing Moon	
Life cycles unend	Waning Moon	
From death in the winter	Winter	**middle circle:** Represents the cycles of nature and the seasons as well as the cycles of birth, death, and rebirth.
To new life in spring	Spring	
Through growth in the summer	Summer	
To decline in the fall	Fall	
From chaos comes order	Athame	**inner circle:** Represents the boundary between you and the rest of the universe.
Metal balanced by wood	Wand	
Creation	Deosil	
Destruction	Widdershins	
Equilibrium's center	You	**center:** Represents the conscious thought that guides your interactions within the universe.
Balance understood		

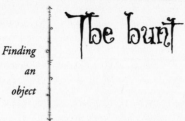

The hunt

The hunt for lost car keys is just as valid as tramping into the woods to hunt game.

Required stones:

* God
* Wand
* Candle
* Winter
* Summer
* Athame
* Sun
* Deosil
* Pentacle
* Spring
* Autumn

Create your magic circle and prepare your layout space.

Place the God stone into its position at the center of your layout area. This stone forms the body of the hunter and all of the other stones are positioned relative to this one. As you lay the stone in place, speak these words of dedication (or similar words of your own) to the God in his role as God of the Hunt.

To the God of the Hunt,
So that all may go well,
I dedicate this ritual,
I cast now this spell.

After you have dedicated this ritual to the God, you should proceed to ask him for his assistance. Place the Sun stone into position as the head of the hunter. With the stone in position, speak the words of request, written below.

From the God of the Hunt,
For assistance I ask.
Please grant me this favor,
Success in my task.

Once you have asked the God for his assistance, you should next invoke the God's energy by reciting the following invocation while placing the Wand stone and then the Deosil stone into their proper positions.

With wand, movement deosil,
Gather energy round.

Since objects belong in the physical realm, a physical change, whether in place or time, etc., depending on the item, will be necessary to find the article you seek. As you place them in their positions as the legs of the hunter, invoke the Candle stone to represent fire (change) and the Pentacle stone to represent earth (the physical world) with the following invocation:

With fire and earth,
My desire be found.

Because the sun is the physical representation of the God, the cycles of the seasons are under his domain. We acknowledge this relationship by reciting the invocation below while placing the four season stones (Winter, Spring, Summer, and Autumn) in their locations, as shown in the diagram.

Controller of seasons,
My prize I will win.

The athame is an instrument of command and direction. While placing the Athame stone into its place in the right hand of the Hunter, invoke it to guide your hunt by speaking the following words:

Direct now my search,
Let the hunt now begin!

Pick up the God stone and, after observing a moment of respectful silence, reflection, and gratitude for his assistance, put the God stone away. Pick up and put away the rest of the witching stones and then disperse your magic space in your usual manner.

Basic love spell

The love spells that follow all require these stones, in the same layout (see page 122), in addition to the stones necessary for the particular spell you are performing. Furthermore, these spells are all performed with the crafter facing north.

Required stones:
* Chalice
* Pentacle
* Goddess
* Censer
* God
* Candle
* Deosil

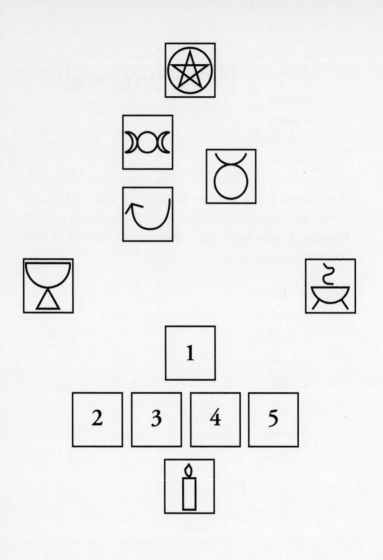

Prepare your layout space. When you have finished, place the Pentacle stone first. It is placed at the top of the layout, in the north. Now place the Censer stone into its proper position on the right, in the east. Next, the Candle stone and then the Chalice stone are placed. These four stones mark the boundaries wherein the rest of the stones are to be placed. After the Chalice stone is placed, speak the following:

With pentacle north, earth invite, be welcome.
With censer at east, air beckon, be welcome.
With candle due south, fire summon, be welcome.
With chalice in west, water gather, be welcome.
Elements attend, elements welcome.

Now place the Goddess stone, God stone, and Deosil stone into the appropriate places. Be sure that you start with the Goddess stone and proceed clockwise around to the Deosil stone. Here these three stones represent the Goddess and the God and their union. When these three have been placed, speak the following:

May the Goddess and God,
By the union they share,
Bestow upon me
Love's blessings, love's care.

At this point you are ready to work any one of the following three love spells.

When you have finished your spell, you may remove the Goddess stone, the God stone, and the Deosil stone. Next remove the Chalice stone, the Candle stone, the Censer stone, and the Pentacle stone. Be sure to remove them in the opposite order from which they were first placed. When this has been done, thank and dismiss the elements with the following words:

> *I give thanks, I am grateful*
> *To the Goddess and God*
> *With the aide of the elements*
> *May you grant love's desires.*

Now disperse your sacred space.

Attracting new love

Follow the basic Love Spell layout.

Required stones:

* ⋆ Waxing Moon
* ⋆ Spring
* ⋆ Wand
* ⋆ Cauldron
* ⋆ Water

Into the position labeled 1 in the Love Spell diagram, place the Waxing Moon stone, symbolizing the Goddess as Maiden. The Spring stone belongs next, in position 2, as spring is when new growth begins. The Wand stone in position 3 represents invocation, the asking. The Cauldron stone and Water stone, in positions 4 and 5, respectively, represent change and purity.

When you have placed all the stones where they belong, take the time to imagine the qualities you would like your new love to have. Avoid being unrealistic in your expectations. When you believe you know what you desire, ask the Goddess to bring the type of person you have in mind into your life. Remember, this spell functions as an invitation to a new love. If you already have strong feelings for a specific person and you want that person to return these feelings, find another way! Magic should never be used in an attempt to sway or manipulate another. When you have finished, remove the five spell stones in reversed order and return to the basic layout procedure.

Strengthening the bonds

*To strengthen
the love
already present
in your life*

Follow the basic Love Spell layout.

Required stones:

- ★ Full Moon
- ★ Summer
- ★ Athame
- ★ Sun
- ★ Salt

Into the position labeled 1 in the Love Spell diagram place the Full Moon stone, which represents the Goddess as Mother. The Summer stone belongs next, in position 2, because summer is a time when all of nature gains strength through growth. The Athame stone in position 3 is a symbol of direction, and the Sun stone and Salt stone, in positions 4 and 5, respectively, are symbolic of strength and earthy, motherly, or familial love.

When you have placed all of the stones where they belong, take the time and call to mind all of the people in your life that you wish to keep close to your heart. See them gathered together around you in a circle, holding hands, with you being the beginning and the end of the circle. When you have the image firmly in mind, picture the love you feel as energy running down your hands and into the people in your circle. Let it flow around and through them, filling up all of the empty spaces in between. Do this for as long as you can maintain the visualization. When you have finished, rest a moment, then remove the five spell stones in reversed order and return to the basic layout procedure.

Note: This spell can be performed with or without the people of your circle present and taking active part in the ritual.

Rekindling a fading spark

To fan the flames of an established love

Follow the basic Love Spell layout.

Required stones:

* ⋆ Waning Moon
* ⋆ Autumn
* ⋆ Balefire
* ⋆ Rebirth
* ⋆ Herbs

Into the position labeled 1 in the Love Spell diagram place the Waning Moon stone, signifying the Goddess as Crone. The Autumn stone belongs next, in position 2. Fall is when the world prepares for the long sleep of winter. It is also the time when trees produce their most glorious displays. The Balefire stone in position 3 symbolizes the small spark being fanned into a roaring blaze, and the Rebirth stone and Salt stone, in positions 4 and 5, respectively, are symbolic of the renewal of desire and the spicing up of your union.

When you have placed all of the stones in their proper places, bring to mind all of the things that brought the two of you together. Remember how it felt to be together in the beginning. Remember the touches, the smells, and the sensations of being together. Feel your desire calling to your partner; picture your partner feeling the love and desire you feel and responding. Do this for as long as you can keep the visualization firmly in mind. When you have finished, remove the five spell stones in reversed order and return to the basic layout procedure.

Drawing a protective circle

This spell is for the creation of a ring of protective energy around oneself, to keep out malicious or harmful energies. If the circle's protection is to be shared with another person, then the other person should remain within the circle, touching the caster, at all times.

Required stones:

- ⋆ Besom
- ⋆ Balefire
- ⋆ Athame
- ⋆ Altar
- ⋆ Wand

Place the Besom stone on the ground approximately 18 inches (45 cm) in front of your toes. Place the Altar stone on the ground between your feet and the Balefire stone on the ground approximately 18 inches (45 cm) behind your heels. Stand upright and hold the Wand stone in your left hand. Hold the Athame stone in your right hand. Now raise your left hand, still clenching the stone, above your head and speak these words:

I call out for Goddess and God
I ask for divinities fair
I stretch out my hand for your guidance
Please aid me with wisdom and care.

As you do this, feel the energy of the Goddess around you. Visualize this energy as a slowly coalescing ball of light around your upraised hand. Let the energy flow down your arm and into you. Feel the energy fill you. When you feel you've received sufficient energy, use your right hand and point the Athame stone at the ground approximately 3.5 feet in front of you. Release the energy and feel it pouring from your left fist, down through your body, along your right arm, and out through your clenched fist and Athame stone like a beam of light aimed at the ground. Slowly begin to turn in a deosil (clockwise) circle. As you turn, use this beam to draw a circle of force around yourself. When you have returned to your starting position, speak the following incantation:

Around and bound
My circle I cast
Against all harm
It shall hold fast.

Draw this circle three times around. Each time you complete the circuit, your circle gains more energy from you. You should be visualizing your circle glowing brighter as you move. Each time you return to your starting position, repeat the incantation.

To disperse the circle follow the same procedure you used to cast it. However, this time, turn widdershins (counter-clockwise) to erase your circle. Each time you return to your starting position, speak these words to your circle:

Around, unbound
My circle disperse
Your energy returned
To the free universe.

When you have done this, pick up and put away the witching stones.

Advanced Spells

Protecting the home

Protects your space from negative energies

To be performed just before moonrise on the three consecutive evenings leading up to the night of the new moon.

Required stones:

- ★ Water
- ★ Deosil
- ★ Widdershins
- ★ Altar
- ★ Salt
- ★ Bane

Other requirements:

- ★ 1 iron nail

   IRON NAIL

Find a quiet place where moonlight will fall upon your layout throughout the night. Stand facing the east and prepare your layout space.

Once you have prepared your space, place your Altar stone on the surface in front of you, in the most western position (closest to you), with the Widdershins stone above it and the Bane stone above that, as shown in the diagram. Now place the Water stone in the most northern position (on your left). The Deosil stone is placed next. It belongs in the most eastern position (farthest from you). The Salt stone is then placed in the most southern position (on your right) and, finally, the iron nail is placed in the center of the layout.

As the moon rises, pass your left hand over your layout from east to west while visualizing the energies moving through the iron nail. Say the following incantation:

O waning moon, thy light I take
With salt, with water, for purity's sake
With altar as anchor, this rod, my stake
A conduit for sorrows and banes I make.
With salt and water and divine moonlight
A conduit for cleansing I create this night.

After you have spoken the incantation, pass your right hand over the layout from east to west while continuing the visualization. When you can no longer hold the image, release it and spend a few moments in quite meditation. Leave your layout set up and repeat this process every evening at moonrise until the night of the new moon.

On the night of the new moon, remove all the stones from around the iron nail. Be sure to start with the Altar stone, Bane stone, and Widdershins stone, and remove the rest in a widdershins (counterclockwise) manner. Then you may disperse your sacred space.

Next, bury the nail in the backyard with the point facing the sky (if you do not have a backyard available, a small container with soil in it placed on a shelf within the home will suffice—just be sure to change the soil occasionally). Visualize the nail attracting negative energies, acting as a lightning rod and channeling them into the earth. Once there, they are dispersed, becoming harmless. As you bury the iron nail, repeat the following incantation three times:

I bury this rod
I begin the flow
Into the earth
Negative energies go.

After you have spoken the incantation three times, continue the visualization for as long as you are able to. When you can no longer hold the image, release it and thank the deities for their generosity and kindness.

Note: Change the soil in the container on the night of a waning or new moon.

To change the soil, remove the nail and empty the used dirt into a suitable container. Add fresh soil to the original container and replant the nail in the fresh soil, following the burial procedure from the end of the original ritual.

To dispose of the used dirt, scatter it by handfuls on the ground in a place where it can be absorbed into the earth. As you scatter each handful, repeat the last two lines of the burial incantation. Rinse your hands and the container that held the used dirt with water, which has had a pinch of salt added to it. Take a moment to visualize the negative energies being absorbed by the earth and dispersed. Now thank the Goddess and the God, and you are finished.

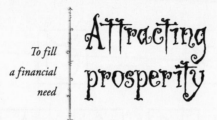

*To fill
a financial
need*

Attracting prosperity

To be done beneath the waxing moon, preferably in the autumn.

Required stones:

- ⋆ Goddess
- ⋆ Salt
- ⋆ Candle
- ⋆ Waxing Moon
- ⋆ Autumn
- ⋆ Censer

- ⋆ God
- ⋆ Wand
- ⋆ Water
- ⋆ Deosil
- ⋆ Herbs
- ⋆ Balefire

Have at hand one piece of paper currency, of a denomination appropriate to the amount you wish to have your prosperity increased by. In U.S. funds: a $1 or $5 bill represents gradual increases, while a $10 or $20 bill represents a single lump sum. Fold the bill (or a check) into thirds along its length. Be sure your creases are tight enough to keep the bill from unfolding. If you don't want to have your money tied up for the length of time required by the spell, then writing a check to yourself also works.

Prepare your layout space. When you have finished, follow the directions below.

Think about what it would take to bring prosperity into your life. Will it require a raise at work? Will more customers for your business bring about prosperity? What

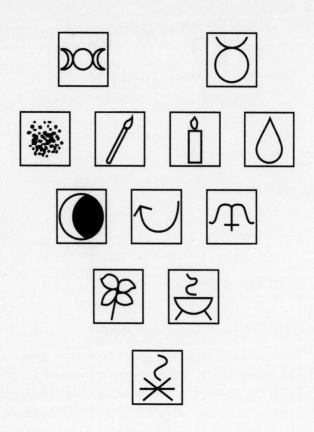

would it take in your life to attain this goal? Concentrate on this as you lay out the required stones in the manner shown in the diagram. When you have the stones spread out before you lay the folded bill on top of the stones and speak the following invocation:

> *I call to the Goddess, I call to the God.*
> *I call to the elements: air, water, earth, fire.*
> *Beneath waxing moon, I gather and harvest.*
> *With herbs, honor Goddess; with censer, the God.*
> *With balefire's bountiful, prosperity mine.*

Leave the stone layout set up.

Come back the following night and unfold one fold of the bill. As you lay the bill back onto the stones, repeat the final line of the invocation.

Come back the following night and unfold the final fold of the bill. As you once again lay the bill back onto the stones, repeat the final line of the invocation.

Leave the stones with the now-unfolded bill lying undisturbed for three nights. On the third night, return to the layout and repeat the entire invocation. Now pick up the bill, refold it, and place it in your pocket.

If it is currency, carry it in your pocket or on your person for a minimum of three days. If it's a check, then carry it in your pocket until such time as you can cash it.

Thank the deities and elements for their assistance and disperse your sacred space. You are done.

Discouraging attention

Perform this spell first thing in the morning.

Required stones:

- ★ Goddess
- ★ Waning Moon
- ★ Cauldron
- ★ Sun
- ★ Altar

Other requirements:

- ★ 1 heat-resistant saucer, actual cauldron, or other similar vessel
- ★ 1 blue candle, in a holder
- ★ 1 2 by 2-inch piece of white paper
- ★ 1 lit taper candle, lighter, or pack of matches

**BLUE
CANDLE**

SAUCER

When you awake in the morning, prepare your layout space. Be sure to be facing south when performing this ritual.

Place the blue candle as close to the southern edge of your layout space as you can. Be sure that it stands within your layout circle. Write your name on one side of the piece of paper and the name of the person whose attentions you want to discourage on the other side. Next, fold the paper diagonally in half so that the other person's name is on the outside and your name is on the inside, then place the paper in the saucer and set them down in the position shown in the layout diagrams. Lay the stones out according to the diagram.

With your taper, lighter, or matches, light the blue candle. As you do so, speak these words of invocation:

Fire, I call forth your energy's ray
Please guide and assist my endeavor this day.

Visualize the light from your candle illuminating an open door and know that the person whose attention you want to discourage stands framed within it. When you have this image firmly in mind, take the folded paper from the saucer and hold one corner up to the candle flame. As the paper catches fire, speak these words and set the burning paper back down on the saucer.

Fire's energy,
Scattered ash,
That unwanted attentions,
Unanswered, will pass.

While the paper burns into ash, close your eyes and picture the door closing, concealing you from the eyes of the other person. Allow the door to close completely, then let the image fade away and open your eyes. If the paper has not burned out, let it do so.

Dip your finger into the ashes in the saucer and draw the bane symbol on your forehead. Next, divide the remaining ashes into four equal portions and, one at a time, place them in the palm of one hand and blow them away to the four compass points. Wipe the ashes from your forehead.

At this time, offer thanks to fire for its assistance. As you say these words, extinguish the candle:

Fire, I release your energy's ray
Your assistance and guidance were welcome this day.

Put away the witching stones and disperse your sacred space. Go about the rest of your day.

Reopening doors of love

This spell is to be performed by two people that are kept together by love and who are held apart by anger.

Required stones:

- ★ Goddess
- ★ Altar
- ★ God
- ★ Cauldron

Other requirements:

- ★ 2 yellow candles, in holder
- ★ 1 2 by 2-inch piece of white paper
- ★ 2 identical, small squares of silk or other suitable fabric
- ★ 1 red ribbon
- ★ 1 blue ribbon
- ★ 1 pink ribbon
- ★ 1 heat-resistant saucer
- ★ 1 writing implement (pen, pencil, other)
- ★ 1 lit taper candle, pack of matches, or lighter

YELLOW   YELLOW
CANDLE   CANDLE

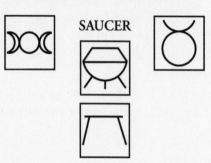

SAUCER

Prepare yourself for bed in your accustomed manner, and then prepare your layout space. Be sure to stand next to each other, facing south, when performing this ritual.

Place the two yellow candles as close to the southern edge of your layout space as possible. Be sure that they stand within your layout circle.

Write your name on one side of the piece of paper and then have your partner write her/his name on the other side. Next, fold the paper diagonally in half. Hand the folded paper to your partner and have her/him fold the paper again to form a small triangle.

Pick up the saucer, then have your partner place the folded paper into the saucer and set them down in the position shown in the layout diagram. Lay the stones out according to the diagram.

With your taper, lighter, or matches, light the yellow candle in front of your partner. As you do so, speak the words of invocation:

Fire, I call forth your energy's light
Please guide and assist our endeavor this night.

Have your partner light the candle in front of you and speak the same invocation.

Each of you then visualize the light from your candle illuminating a closed door, and know that your partner waits just beyond. When you both have this image firmly in mind, take the folded paper from the saucer and hold one corner up to the candle flame in front of your partner. As the paper catches fire, both of you speak these words, together, as you set the burning paper back into the saucer:

Fire's energy
Mingled ash
Through door of destiny
My form and my match.

While the paper burns, turn toward each other and both of you close your eyes. Picture the doors opening up to reveal yourselves to each other. Imagine the love that holds you together as a visible light—see this light reaching out from both of you toward each other through the open doorway. As your love merges, allow the image to fade from your minds and open your eyes to see each other. If the paper has not already burned out, continue to gaze at each other until it does.

When you have finished gazing at each other, each of you dip a finger into the ashes in the saucer and draw the appropriate symbol on your partner's forehead. If your partner is female, draw the Waxing Moon symbol; if male, draw the Horned God symbol.

Next, divide the remaining ashes into two equal portions. Each of you wrap a portion in the silk cloths to make two small bundles. Tie the bundles with either the pink or blue ribbons, depending on the gender of your partner.

Now tie the two bundles together with the red ribbon. You tie one knot and your partner ties a second knot. Set them down in the saucer.

At this time, offer silent thanks to fire for its assistance. As you both say these words, together, extinguish the two yellow candles:

Fire, we release your energy's light
Your assistance and guidance were welcome this night.

Put away the witching stones and disperse your sacred space. Place the tied package in a shared space, like a dresser or closet or even between the mattress, and go to bed.

Creating a lucky stone

This spell is for the creation of a charm that will attract positive energy to the person who carries it.

Required stones:

- ★ Altar
- ★ Candle
- ★ Salt
- ★ God

- ★ Censer
- ★ Water
- ★ Goddess
- ★ Athame

Other requirements:

- ★ 1 small cat's-eye stone or 1 small stone of your choice

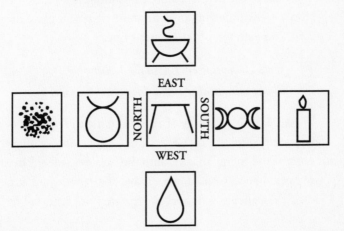

Draw your circle and, while facing east, prepare your layout space.

When you are ready, gather your energies and concentrate on the ritual you are about to perform. Lay the chips out as shown in the diagram. Begin with the Altar stone. Then place the Goddess stone beside the Altar stone, followed by the God stone, each to their respective sides.

Now place the Censer, Candle, Water, and Salt stones into their proper positions and in the specified order.

Pick up the cat's-eye stone and, while speaking the following invitations to the Goddess and the God, place the cat's-eye stone upon the Altar stone.

To the Goddess I issue this invitation,
Please stand as a witness to this consecration.
For the God, this invitation I now intone,
Please witness my ritual, the transformation of stone.

Wait a few moments in respectful silence, until you feel the presence of the deities, before continuing.

Now say the following invocation to air as you place the cat's-eye stone on top of the Censer stone.

To elemental air I send forth this plea,
Please witness this circle, lend energy to me.

Visualize the blue energy of air enveloping the two stones and flowing into the cat's-eye stone. Allow only a small amount of the energy to enter into the cat's-eye stone. Place your open hand, palm down, above the stones and say, "Hold." Visualize the flow of energy stopping and fading out.

After the energy flow has subsided, speak the following invocation to Fire as you pick up the cat's-eye stone and set it down upon the Candle stone.

To elemental fire I make this appeal,
Please witness this circle, lend energy to me.

Visualize the red energy of fire rising from the Candle stone and entering the cat's-eye stone. Again, allow only that portion of fire's energy needed to balance the energy from air to enter the stone. Stop the inflow of energy in the same manner as you did for air, and let the excess sink back into the Candle stone.

When you are ready, pick up the cat's-eye stone and set it down on the Water stone. As you do so, speak the following invocation to water:

To elemental water I present this petition,
Please witness this circle, lend energy to me.

Visualize the translucent shimmer of water's energy coalescing in an aura around the two stones, and begin its flow into the cat's-eye stone. Again, try to balance the input of water's energy with the energy from air. Stop the energy flow in exactly the same manner as you did previously and see the energy flow stop and the aura disperse.

Now speak the invocation to earth as you pick up the cat's-eye stone and set it down on the Salt stone.

To elemental earth I ask this request,
Please witness this circle, lend energy to me.

Visualize energy in colors of the earth (greens, brown, etc.) concentrating around the two stones and moving into the cat's-eye stone. When the energy from earth is balanced with the rest, again stretch out your hand and stop the movement, as you did before, and allow the energy to melt away.

Pick up the cat's-eye stone and, in silence, return the stone to its starting point on the Altar stone. Now, gather your personal energy and concentrate on creating a positive energy attracter. When you feel yourself energized and focused, pick up the Athame stone and hold it tightly in your hand above the cat's-eye stone and the Altar stone. Speak the following words to charge your stone with purpose:

> *Stone with energies now endowed*
> *With my energy and purpose found*
> *Now your energies to my purpose bound.*

Feel your energy flow from yourself, through the Athame stone and into the cat's-eye stone. Use your energy to bring the elemental energies together and bind them to the purpose of attracting positive energy (luck). When this has been accomplished, stop your energy flow and release it.

Take a moment to rest from your exertion, and then use the following incantations to thank and release the elements. As you speak these words, pick up the appropriate witching stone from your layout and put it away.

AIR (Censer stone)
> *I send forth thanks to elemental air*
> *For energies asked for and received*
> *Go as you will, my purpose now achieved.*

FIRE (Candle stone)

I offer thanks to elemental fire
For energies asked for and received
Go as you will, my purpose now achieved.

WATER (Water stone)

I present my thanks to elemental water
For energies asked for and received
Go as you will, my purpose now achieved.

EARTH (Salt stone)

I voice my thanks to elemental earth
For energies asked for and received
Go as you will, my purpose now achieved.

After you have given thanks to the elements, offer thanks to the Goddess for her blessings and then to the God for his with the following words:

I offer my thanks to the Goddess perpetual,
For standing as witness to this evening's ritual.
To the God, my thanks, forbearance you've shown,
In the witnessing of this, my transformation of stone.

At this time you should put away the Goddess stone and then the God stone. Now, pick up the cat's-eye stone and place it in a pocket. It should always be kept on the right-hand side of your body.

Put away the Altar stone and disperse your sacred space.

THE CRAFT

A Witch's Book of Shadows

DOROTHY MORRISON

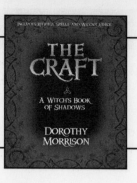

Teaching newcomers how to
begin the path of the Witch

So, you want to be a Witch. You've read everything you can get your hands on about spells and magic, but you're still asking yourself, "How do I begin?"

The Craft answers that question, and so many more. Beginning with the basics of the Wiccan religion and its practices, this book moves forward with easy-to-follow instructions for working with major power sources like the deities and elements. You'll discover the importance of magical boosters, and find out how to get the most from their power. You'll travel the path of ritual tools, and learn to make, obtain, and use them to their best advantage. Then it's off to circle-casting and all it has to offer. Afterward, you'll explore the realm of the Esbats, the Sabbats, and the party-hardy world of ritual celebration. Everything you need for successful witchery is here, including mental theory, magical theory, and practical training exercises.

1-56718-446-4
7½ x 9⅛, 240 pp., illus. $14.95

To order, call 1-877-NEW-WRLD
Prices subject to change without notice

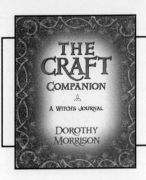

THE CRAFT COMPANION
A Witch's Journal

DOROTHY MORRISON

Craft your own Book of Shadows

Start your own Book of Shadows with this companion guide to *The Craft*. *The Craft Companion's* journal-like format with lined pages gives you plenty of room for your own magical notes and planning. A unique assortment of more than 100 short spells and affirmations, one per each journal page, are designed to spark creativity and further you along the spiritual path. Also includes the Wiccan Rede.

> *For success on contracts signed—*
> *Or written papers of any kind—*
> *Turn the papers all facedown*
> *And with each one a pentacle crown*
> *Just lick your finger and then draw*
> *Then bind the spell with Karmic Law*

0-7387-0093-2
7½ x 9⅛, 240 pp. $14.95

To order, call 1-877-NEW-WRLD
Prices subject to change without notice

TO RIDE A SILVER BROOMSTICK

New Generation Witchcraft

SILVER RAVENWOLF

Throughout the world there is a new generation of Witches—people practicing or wishing to practice the Craft on their own, without an in-the-flesh magickal support group. *To Ride a Silver Broomstick* speaks to those people, presenting them with both the science and religion of Witchcraft, allowing them to become active participants while growing at their own pace. It is ideal for anyone: male or female, young or old, those familiar with Witchcraft, and those totally new to the subject and unsure of how to get started.

Full of the author's warmth, humor, and personal anecdotes, *To Ride a Silver Broomstick* leads you step-by-step through the various lessons with exercises and journal writing assignments. This is the complete Witchcraft 101, teaching you to celebrate the Sabbats, deal with coming out of the broom closet, choose a magickal name, visualize the Goddess and God, meditate, design a sacred space, acquire magickal tools, design and perform rituals, network, spell cast, perform color and candle magick, divination, healing, telepathy, psychometry, astral projection, and much, much more.

0-87542-791-X
7 x 10, 320 pp., illus. $14.95

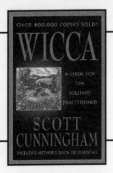

WICCA

A Guide for the Solitary Practitioner

SCOTT CUNNINGHAM

Wicca is a book of life, and how to live magically, spiritually, and wholly attuned with Nature. It is a book of sense and common sense, not only about Magick, but about religion and one of the most critical issues of today: how to achieve the much needed and wholesome relationship with our Earth. Cunningham presents Wicca as it is today: a gentle, Earth-oriented religion dedicated to the Goddess and God. This book fulfills a need for a practical guide to solitary Wicca—a need which no previous book has fulfilled.

Here is a positive, practical introduction to the religion of Wicca, designed so that any interested person can learn to practice the religion alone, anywhere in the world. It presents Wicca honestly and clearly, without the pseudo-history that permeates other books. It shows that Wicca is a vital, satisfying part of modern life.

0-87542-118-0
6 x 9, 240 pp., illus. $9.95

Also available in Spanish
Wicca: Una guía para la práctica individual
0-7387-0306-0 US $14.95 CAN $22.95

To order, call 1-877-NEW-WRLD
Prices subject to change without notice

TEEN WITCH

Wicca for a New Generation

SILVER RAVENWOLF

Teenagers and young adults comprise a growing market for books on Witchcraft and magick, yet there has never been a book written specifically for the teen seeker. Now, Silver RavenWolf, one of the most well-known Wiccans today and the mother of four young Witches, gives teens their own handbook on what it takes and what it means to be a Witch. Humorous and compassionate, *Teen Witch* gives practical advice for dealing with everyday life in a magickal way. From homework and crabby teachers to parents and dating, this book guides teens through the ups and downs of life as they move into adulthood. Spells are provided that address their specific concerns, such as the "Call Me Spell" and "The Exam Spell."

Parents will also find this book informative and useful as a discussion tool with their children. Discover the beliefs of Witchcraft, Wiccan traditions, symbols, holidays, rituals, and more.

1-56718-725-0
7 x 10, 288 pp. $12.95

TEEN WITCH KIT
Silver RavenWolf

Everything You Need to Make Magick!

Here is everything the novice spellcaster needs to practice the Craft of the Wise—and be a force for good. Step into the sacred space and discover the secrets of one of the world's oldest mysteries: the art and science of white magick, a gentle, loving practice. The kit contains a beautifully illustrated book of instruction, plus six magickal talismans, salt, and a spell bag. The kit box converts into your own personal altar.

The quick reading guidebook, complete with instructions on how to prepare yourself for magick, create a sacred space, call up the spirit, and draw down the Moon. All the spells are tailored to 13- to 18-year-olds, and can be cast using the items in the kit and common objects found around the house. It's easy to follow the step-by-step instructions and clear magickal symbols. There is even a section on how to write your own spells.

1-56718-554-1 $24.95

7½ x 7½ boxed kit contains: 128-pp. illus. book • spell bag • spell salt • golden coin • silver wish cord • silver bell • natural quartz crystal • silver pentacle pendant • yes/no coin

MAGICK & RITUALS
OF THE MOON
EDAIN MCCOY

Harness the energy of "Lady Luna"

(Formerly titled *Lady of the Night.*) Moon-centered ritual, a deeply woven thread in Pagan culture, is often confined to celebration of the full moon. Edain McCoy revitalizes the full potential of the lunar mysteries in this exclusive guide for Pagans.

Magick & Rituals of the Moon explores the lore, rituals, and unique magickal potential associated with all phases of the moon: full, waxing, waning, moonrise/moonset, and dark/new. Combined with an in-depth look at moon magick and rituals, this book offers a complete system for riding the tides of lunar magick.

Written for both solitary and group practice, *Magick & Rituals of the Moon* breaks new ground by showing how both men and women can Draw Down the Moon for enhanced spirituality. Pagans will find fun and spirited suggestions on how to make the mystery of the moon accessible to non-Pagans through creative party planning and popular folklore.

0-7387-0092-4
7 x 10, 256 pp. $14.95